spectacular walls!

Jeannine Dostal

NORTH LIGHT BOOKS
Cincinnati, Ohio
www.artistsnetwork.com

Spectacular Walls!: Creative Effects Using Texture, Embellishment and Paint. Copyright © 2005 by Jeannine Dostal. Manufactured in China. All rights reserved. No part of this book may be reproduced in any form or by any electronic or mechanical means including information storage and retrieval systems without permission in writing from the publisher, except by a reviewer who may quote brief passages in a review. Published by North Light Books, an imprint of F+W Publications, Inc., 4700 East Galbraith Road, Cincinnati, Ohio 45236. (800) 289-0963. First edition.

Distributed in Canada by Fraser Direct
100 Armstrong Avenue
Georgetown, ON, Canada L7G 554

Distributed in the U.K. and Europe by David & Charles
Brunel House, Newton Abbot, Devon, TQ12 4PU, England
Tel: (+44) 1626 323200, Fax: (+44) 1626 323319
Email: mail@davidandcharles.co.uk

Distributed in Australia by Capricorn Link
P.O. Box 704, Windsor, NSW 2756 Australia

Other fine North Light Books are available from your local bookstore, art supply store or direct from the publisher.

09 08 07 06 05   5 4 3 2 1

Library of Congress Cataloging-in-Publication Data

Dostal, Jeannine
  Spectacular walls! : creative effects using texture, embellishment and paint / Jeannine Dostal.
    p. cm.
  Includes index.
  ISBN 1-58180-727-9 (pbk. : alk. paper)
  1. House painting. 2. Interior decoration. 3. Texture Painting
    I. Title.
  TT323 .D68 2005
  747 .3-dc22

                                                2005005948

Editor: Christina D. Read
Production Coordinator: Kristen Heller
Cover Designer: Clare Finney
Graphic Designers: Cindy Stanard & Clare Finney
Photographers: Christine Polomsky & Tim Grondin
Photo Stylist: Nora Martini

fW
F+W PUBLICATIONS, INC.

Metric Conversion Chart

To convert	to	multiply by
Inches	Centimeters	2.54
Centimeters	Inches	0.4
Feet	Centimeters	30.5
Centimeters	Feet	0.03
Yards	Meters	0.9
Meters	Yards	1.1
Sq. Inches	Sq. Centimeters	6.45
Sq. Centimeters	Sq. Inches	0.16
Sq. Feet	Sq. Meters	0.09
Sq. Meters	Sq. Feet	10.8
Sq. Yards	Sq. Meters	0.8
Sq. Meters	Sq. Yards	1.2
Pounds	Kilograms	0.45
Kilograms	Pounds	2.2
Ounces	Grams	28.3
Grams	Ounces	0.035

Jeannine Dostal

Jeannine Dostal has always had a love for design and art. After graduating from the University of Cincinnati's fashion design program, her first job took her to India where she designed beaded and sequined gowns. Other design jobs included work in graphics and embroidery.

In the early 1990s, Jeannine began her work with faux finishes. She received extensive training from Faux Effects International, Prismatic Painting Studio, The Finishing School and countless other classes. She also learned the art of authentic fresco painting from the School of Adam in Nice, France.

Jeannine teaches her techniques in seminars and conventions throughout the United States, and her work has been published in national faux-finishing magazines. For further information, visit her Web site, www.jeanninedostal.com.

For the loves of my life: my husband, Keith; my parents, Bill and Nancy Cleary; my siblings, Mike, Lynne, Jack and their families and the Dostals.

Thank you to the universe for letting the following people enter and influence my life at the exact right moment:

To my sister, Lynne—thanks for introducing me to the works of artist Gustav Klimt. To my husband, Keith; parents, Bill and Nancy and brothers, Jack and Mike—thank you for love, support and shoulders. Thank you to wonderful designers—Meg Fiora, Nimbus Nine (Mindy, Susie, Amy), René Graham and Becky Schnell—for believing in me and pushing me way beyond my self-limitations. Thank you to Ray Sandor, Jane Koehler, Jodie Baldanza and Lisa Chubb from Faux Effects for giving me the tools and support to become a professional. Thanks to Gary Lord, my mentor, for the recommendation of this very book! Thanks to my girlfriends Meg, Marla, Judy, M.B., Mindy E., Susan, Margaret, Amy and all my lake buddies. Thank you to each and every one of my clients. Special thanks to the Bandys, Borgmans, Brauns, Courtneys, Fishers, Shelbys, Thamens, Tomasics, Williams, Zinks, Ambience Salon and Montgomery Inn Ribs King for generously opening up your homes and businesses for the photos in this book. Thank you F+W: Chris Read, Kathy Kipp, Christine Polomsky, Holly Davis, Jamie Markle and Clare Finney for making this a "spectacular" experience. And to my readers—thank you!

contents

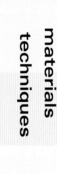

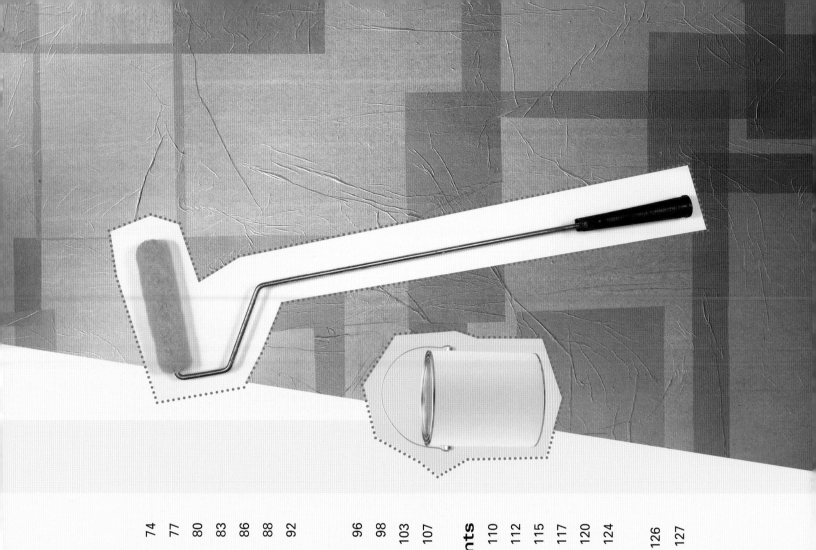

materials

paints

Latex Paint

Throughout this book you will find that I use Porter brand latex paint for basecoats, glazes and drywall mud mixes. I know their colors well and I love their low-sheen qualities. However, you can use any brand of latex paint for your own projects.

Water-Based Metallic Paint

I love the Modern Masters color selection of metallic paints. I use them to make beautiful glazes. (See Resources on page 126 for more information.)

Acrylic Paint

I use all brands of acrylic paints. These small bottled paints are handy for everything from painting murals to making glazes. They can be purchased at most craft and hobby stores.

Squeeze Bottle Paint

I use various types of 3-D paints. They come in pearlized, sparkle and matte colors and can be purchased at most craft and hobby stores.

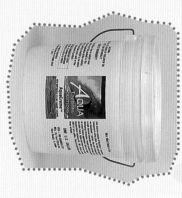

Glaze

I only use Faux Effects glazes. My usual choice is AquaGlaze from the Aqua line. This glaze is not only wonderful to work with, but it stays open (wet) longer than any glaze I have used. You can mix AquaGlaze with any water-based metallic, latex or acrylic paint. Use it once and you'll be hooked.

AquaCreme

You'll love AquaCreme, too. AquaCreme is from the Faux Effects Aqua line and can only be used over Faux Effects Aqua base products. Also, you can only tint AquaCreme with tints from the Faux Effects Aqua line.

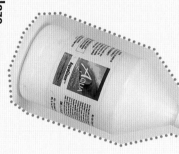

AquaTint

AquaTints by Faux Effects are used to tint AquaCreme. I also use them to tint DecoArt Sandstones. (See Resources on page 126 for information on where to purchase Faux Effects and DecoArt products.)

AquaStone

AquaStone by Faux Effects can be used to create an endless variety of textured surfaces.

DecoArt Sandstones

This product comes in various colors. I love the way it trowels, brushes or rolls onto the wall. When dry, it has a slight sparkle finish. DecoArt Sandstones can be found at most craft and hobby stores or through the DecoArt Web site (see Resources on page 126).

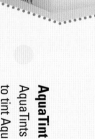

Gel Medium

Gel medium is another product used to create textured surfaces. I mix it with latex paint for a smooth texture, or I add all-purpose sand for added dimension on walls. Gel medium can be found at craft, hobby and specialty paint stores.

Joint Compound

I love using joint compound and paint mixed together. You don't need to basecoat, and it glazes beautifully; the colors melt into each other. I use Rapid-Bond joint compound. Always use 90 set, because it will stay open (wet and workable) for longer periods of time. *Always* mix this powder *into* the latex paint. You can find joint compound at any major hardware store and in many paint stores.

Cake Decorating Tools

Cake decorating bags and assorted tips can be used to add dimensional treatments to walls. These can be purchased at craft, hobby and grocery stores.

Liquitex Modeling Paste

This product is used to model 3-D objects, as in the "Trailing Dimensional Ivy" project (see page 58). It can also be used to create all kinds of textured surfaces as well as raised stencils. Purchase it at craft and hobby stores.

Golden Products

I use Golden acrylic metallics for textures and glazes. They can be found at most craft and hobby stores.

other products

Clear Acrylic Spray Varnish

Spray varnish seals the copper leaf in "Revealed Metal" (see page 14). You can find this product in any paint or hardware store. Any brand will do.

Decorative Paper

Specialty art-and-craft tissue, hand-painted paper or handmade paper is an interesting addition to many faux wall treatments. They can be found at art supply, craft, hobby and scrapbooking stores.

Wallpaper Cutouts

Prepasted wallpaper cutouts are a shortcut to creating a fun wall. Just add a jewel here and a sparkle there for your own personal touch. They are available at craft and hobby stores.

Embellishments

I love incorporating beautiful jewels and sparkles into my finishes. They add interest, depth, beauty and fun to any faux finish. Acrylic jewels, marble accents, sparkle glitter, premade roses, pearls, fringe and more can be found at any craft and hobby store.

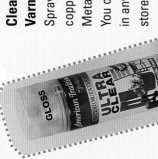

White Craft Glue

When craft glue is mixed with water, it makes a great paste for applying tissue paper. You can find this glue at craft, hobby, grocery and chain stores.

YES! Paste

I learned about this product when I was making a lamp shade and needed a glue that could handle heat. YES! paste also has a thick consistency, and I find it perfect for troweling through stencils because it doesn't run. You'll notice that I use YES! paste for a lot of different purposes.

Stencils

I have been using Royal Design Studio stencils for years. These stencils are by far my favorite. There are so many designs to choose from. NOTE: Be sure you clean your stencils after each use. This makes them last much longer.

Drill & Drill Attachment

Make sure the drill you use is designed for mixing heavy materials. If you try to mix the paint and joint compound by hand, it will be lumpy. Not only is this a pain in the neck, but it will give you a pain in the neck! You need to stir this mixture with a drill and mixing attachment so that it will be blended to a smooth consistency.

Venetian Trowel & Japan Scraper

I'd be lost without my Venetian trowel! It's especially made for plaster finishes, and I use it in various sizes. Once you use this specialty trowel, you'll never use another type.

Japan scrapers are used for troweling thick materials through a stencil. You can order Venetian trowels and Japan scrapers from either Faux Effects or Prismatic Painting Studio (see Resources on page 126). You can also generally find Venetian trowels in large hardware stores.

Cake Mixer

To make up sample mixes of paint and joint compound or for small jobs, I use a very inexpensive hand-held cake mixer. Don't laugh—it works!

Metal & Plastic Trowels

I use metal and plastic trowels for scooping material from a bucket onto my Venetian trowel. These trowels can be purchased at any hardware store.

Combs

I love combing in textured surfaces—it's fun, fast, easy and effective. You can find metal or plastic combs made especially for wood graining at craft, hobby and specialty art stores.

Scissors

I don't go anywhere without a few sets of scissors. I never know when I'll need them. They're used for cutting decorative papers, tissue, etc.

Screwdriver

And you thought this tool was only used for taking off light switch plates! I use a screwdriver to carve into my special joint compound/paint mix. I've tried lots of other things, but this is my favorite tool for "carving."

Chip Brush

I'm a fan of the chip brush! I use it for glazing, striae, murals and countless other techniques. You can find chip brushes at any paint or hardware store.

Sea Sponge

I use a sea sponge to apply textured materials and to manipulate glazes. Beautiful patterns can also be created with a sea sponge. This item can be found at any craft, hobby or paint store.

Staple Gun

Always have a staple gun handy. I use mine to attach fringe and ribbon to walls. Staples are strong and reliable, so embellishments remain securely on the wall.

Other Assorted Products

I use paint roller pans and liners for applying glazes and plastic buckets for mixing glazes. I store leftover paint in inexpensive plastic food containers. Plant misters and spray bottles are perfect for spraying water on works-in-progress, for moving glaze around the wall and for creating special glaze effects.

Artist Brush

Use these brushes for murals, fine-detail painting and applying paste and sparkles. You can purchase a variety of medium-sized acrylic artist paintbrushes at any craft, hobby or specialty art store.

Level

Use a level to check the straightness of my stripes, to make level marks for tissue application, to check that decorative papers are placed straight on a wall and for countless other tasks. Levels are available at any hardware store. I never leave home without it!

Terry Cloth Towel

I use terry cloth towels like they're going out of style! I buy them in packs of 12 or 24. They're fantastic for glazing.

Paint Roller

I like to use small rollers, like a 6-inch (15cm), for applying glazes because they are easy to handle. I usually use the Whizz brand, which is found in most paint or hardware stores.

Tape

I use blue 3M Safe-Release Painters' Masking Tape for taping off trim and holding up stencils. I use the white Safe-Release tape for taping off ceilings and creating stripes, diamonds, etc. directly on drywall—it won't pull off wall paint. You can find this or other comparable brands at most paint and hardware stores.

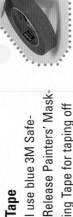

tip

Wash all your chip brushes in a washing machine. Just put the dirty brushes in a lingerie bag and set the wash on delicate. Always air dry your brushes. Don't put them in a dryer!

techniques

tip

Keep a 5-gallon (2dal) bucket filled with water handy. Toss your used chip brushes, terry cloth towels and paint rollers into the water. This keeps paint from drying on your tools and makes cleanup much easier. When you wash the towels, they'll be as good as new.

Drywall Mud/Paint Mix

I developed this mix because I wanted to duplicate the look of European frescoes. I experimented to create the look in an easier and less expensive way than was traditionally done. Years ago, Gary Lord, a decorative painter, gave me the tip of mixing drywall mud and paint together. Once I came up with a formula, I expanded on the ways to use this product by carving designs into it and placing gems and other embellishments into it.

Assemble everything you need to make up your drywall mud/paint mix. The basic formula is approximately 1 cup (2dl) of Rapid-Bond Lite 90 Setting Type Joint Compound powder (always use at least a 90 setting product) to 10-12 ounces (3-4dl) of any latex paint. Remember, this is an approximation. Your finished mix should resemble thick cake batter.

To start, *always* pour paint into your mixing bucket first. Then add the drywall powder at a rate of one to two cups at a time. Then mix—you need to use a drill with a mixing attachment for large quantities of the mix. For small batches you can use an inexpensive kitchen hand mixer. Always make more drywall mud/paint mix than you'll need for your job, and be sure to clean your drill and hand mixer as soon as possible.

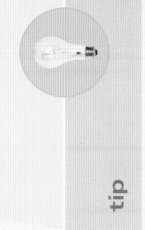

tip

Remember, trying new techniques and tools can be awkward at first. After a little practice, you'll get a natural feel for the process.

Glaze/Paint Mix

In my years of doing decorative painting, I have searched for the best products for my work. I've found the Faux Effects products to be the easiest and best quality. I use AquaGlaze, from the Faux Effects Aqua line, because it is compatible with any latex, acrylic, water-based metallic or other water-based paint.

The basic glaze formula when glazing porous walls is three to four parts glaze to one part paint (depending on climate and the amount of moisture in the air). This allows a longer open time (longer working time before the glaze/paint mix dries). Mix your materials thoroughly in a container with a paint stirring stick.

How to Glaze

The key to glazing on this porous drywall mud/paint mix is as follows: Use a roller with glaze on a 2' x 2' (61cm x 61cm) section of wall. Spread the glaze around with a damp terry cloth towel using sweeping circular and figure-eight motions. Make sure to create an abstract shape on the wall—no hard edges. Feather the edges until

a very little cloudlike glaze is visible. If needed, use a dry terry cloth towel to soften and blend any glaze that the damp towel can't remove.

Start the next section 18" to 24" (46cm to 61cm) away from the last section. Repeat the glazing process and feather the edges into the section just completed. Your glazed shapes should move in and out of each other so that no overlap lines are visible.

To make the glaze move easily, spray with water. This allows the

glaze to slide across and melt into the wall beautifully. Try to practice this technique on a large piece of wallboard until you feel comfortable using it. You'll be pleasantly surprised, however, at how easy this technique is. On a sealed wall (a wall with a satin or semigloss paint finish) I only use a dry towel and do not spray with water.

easier & faster plaster

When you use a creamy color palette, this finish creates a stunning Tuscan finish that's easy, forgiving and fast to do. It also looks spectacular in pale lavenders, soft blues, corals and almost any other soft color combination. You're painting your home—choose the colors you want to live with.

tip

It's important to choose three paint colors that are all variations (light, medium, darker medium) of the same color.

Home of Mr. & Mrs. Martin & Jean Tomasic

Supplies

- Paint roller and pan
- Rapid-Bond Lite 90 Setting Type Joint Compound powder
- Drill and mixing attachment
- Buckets or other containers
- Venetian trowel
- Metal or plastic trowel
- Porter Paint #6704-1 Soft Cloud (satin)
- Porter Paint #6703-1 Queen Anne's Lace (satin)
- Porter Paint #6705-2 Beige Chiffon (satin)

#6704-1*

#6703-1*

#6705-2*

*Color shown as drywall mud/paint mix.

Easier & Faster Plaster

1 Basecoat

Basecoat the walls with Soft Cloud. Let dry 24 hours.

2 Apply drywall mud/paint mix

Make a drywall mud/paint mix (see formula on page 10) of each individual paint color, using Soft Cloud as the main color. Trowel on all three colors simultaneously. Smear the colors in and out of each other—do not overblend to make one solid color. Let dry.

14

revealed metal

This is a spin-off of a finish that Gary Lord, a nationally known decorative painter and good friend, created years ago. The technique is exactly the same as "Easier & Faster Plaster," with the addition of metallic copper showing through the plaster.

Try silver or gold leaf or even a complementary paint color peeking through your revealed plaster!

Home of Bill & Amy Thaman

Supplies

- Paint roller and pan
- Houston Art Metal Leaf Adhesive Size
- Buckets or other containers
- Foam brush
- Houston Art Genuine Copper Metal Leaf
- 2-inch (51mm) chip brush
- Terry cloth towels
- Clear spray acrylic finish
- Rapid-Bond Lite 90 Setting Type Joint Compound powder
- Venetian trowel
- Metal or plastic trowel
- Porter Paint #6121-2 Clear Peach (satin) half-strength formula
- Porter Paint #6123-2 Peach Cloud (satin)

#6123-2*

#6121-2*

*Color shown as drywall mud/paint mix.

tip

When applying size, put pieces of tape on the wall right by the areas where you paint on the size. The tape will remind you where you've applied the clear-drying size.

1 Basecoat

Basecoat the wall with Clear Peach. Let dry 24 hours.

2 Size the walls

Pour the metal leaf size into a separate container. Use a foam brush to apply the size in an even layer and in random areas onto the wall. The size goes on as a milky color and dries clear. Let the size set for about one hour.

3 Apply the copper leaf

Take a sheet of copper leaf out of the book by the corner. Place the sheet onto the sized area of the wall and brush with a dry 2-inch (51mm) chip brush. Use firm pressure on the brush to remove any copper leaf that has not adhered to the wall.

4 Rub copper leafing

Take a damp, clean towel and rub off any loose copper leaf pieces. Vacuum up any copper leaf pieces that may have fallen on the ground.

5 Protect copper leafing

Spray the copper leaf areas with protective acrylic finish. Do this so the copper leafing will not verdigris and change colors—unless you want that effect!

6 Make a drywall mud/paint mix

Make a drywall mud/paint mixture of each color. (see page 10). Trowel your colors onto the wall simultaneously, smearing them in and out of each other. Do not overblend to make one solid color, and be sure to leave copper areas showing.

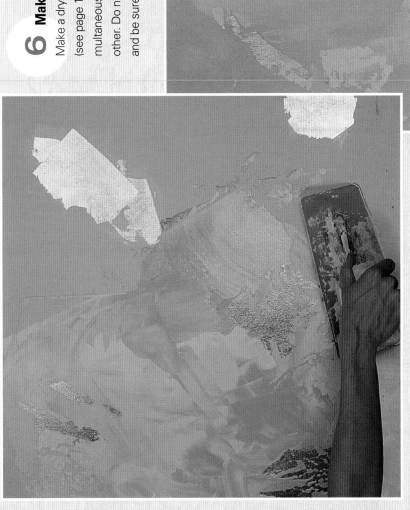

tip

Keep your area clean of any loose leaf. It can create a mess if it gets into your paint finish.

fresco style in a little while

I'm crazy about softly textured and glazed finishes. They remind me of traditional European walls. This drywall mud/paint mix allows the painted overcoat glaze to melt into the surface and duplicate that beautiful fresco look.

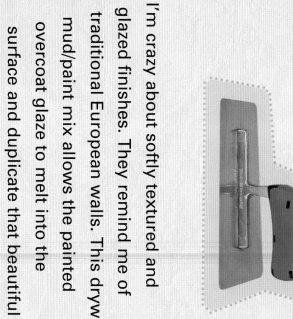

Supplies

- Paint roller and pan
- Rapid-Bond Lite 90 Setting Type Joint Compound powder
- Drill and mixing attachment
- Buckets or other containers
- Venetian trowel
- Metal or plastic trowel
- AquaGlaze
- Terry cloth towels
- Spray bottle with water
- Chip brushes
- Porter Paint #6896-1 Off White (satin)
- Porter Paint #6689-4 Deep Dosinia (satin)

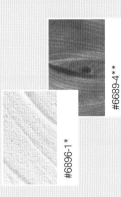

#6896-1*

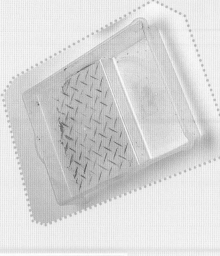

#6689-4**

*Color shown as drywall mud/paint mix.

**Color shown as glaze/paint mix.

1 Basecoat & apply mud/paint mix

Basecoat walls with Off White. Let dry 24 hours. Make a drywall mud/paint mix (see page 10) with the Off White. Trowel the mud/paint mix on the wall. You can create as much or as little texture as you'd like. Thicker areas can crack—this creates an "Old World" finish. Let dry completely.

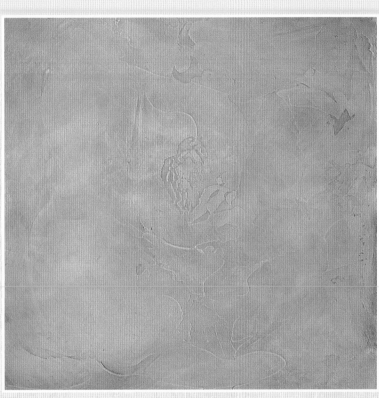

2 Apply the glaze/paint mix

Make up your glaze/paint mix (see page 11) with Deep Dosinia. Apply to the wall with a roller. Immediately start rubbing the mix into the wall finish with a wet terry cloth towel. Make sure to rub off the outside edges to a very sheer finish (see "How to Glaze" on page 11). Use the spray bottle, if necessary, to keep the glaze mixture wet, especially on the outside edges. Use chip brushes to push the glaze into corners and other tight areas.

Fresco Style in a Little While

honeycomb

There is nothing more fun than playing in the mud! Sometimes I have to hold myself back from jumping right in. This technique is fun, easy and fabulous. You can create amazing texture with minimal effort. And since you're the "creative director," you can make your walls as bold or subtle as you like. Spectacular!

Supplies

- Paint rollers and pans
- Rapid-Bond Lite 90 Setting Type Joint Compound powder
- Drill and mixing attachment
- Buckets and other containers
- Venetian trowel
- Metal or plastic trowel
- Metal combs (used for woodgraining)
- AquaGlaze
- 3-inch (76mm) chip brushes
- Terry cloth towels
- Porter Paint #6838-2 Antique Cream (satin)
- Porter Paint #6774-4 Muted Copper (satin)

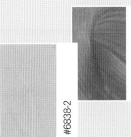

#6838-2

#6774-4*

*Color shown as glaze/paint mix.

1 See previous technique

Basecoat your wall with Antique Cream. Let dry 24 hours. Follow steps 1 and 2 of "Fresco Style in a Little While" (see page 19), using Antique Cream for the drywall mud mix and Muted Copper for the glaze mix.

2 Combing

While the walls are still wet, take a metal comb and drag through the drywall in different directions, all over the area you are working.

3 Smooth the combing

Take the trowel and very lightly smooth over the combing here and there. Let dry overnight.

4 Apply the glaze/paint mix

Make up the glaze/paint mix (see page 11) with Muted Copper. Roll on the glaze/paint mix. Then take your chip brush and scrub the glaze mix into the texture, in the direction of the combing.

5 Remove excess glaze

Take a damp rag and rub into the wall surface, removing the excess glaze (see "How to Glaze" on page 11). Soften with a dry terry cloth towel if needed.

Honeycomb

faux metal

An interior designer I work with put the pressure on—I had to come up with a finish that matched a discontinued wall sample. And the designer needed it yesterday! Voilà—this metallic finish is now a favorite among designers and clients. It is versatile and lends itself to any decor—from contemporary to traditional. This technique is perfect for powder rooms, libraries or any cozy spot.

Supplies

- Paint rollers and pans
- Rapid-Bond Lite 90 Setting Type Joint Compound powder
- Drill and mixing attachment
- Buckets or other containers
- Venetian trowel
- Metal or plastic trowel
- AquaCreme
- 3-inch (76mm) chip brush
- Terry cloth towels
- Porter Paint #6883-1 White Wheat (satin)
- Porter Paint #6838-2 Antique Cream (satin)
- Black AquaColor
- Modern Masters Metallic ME 150 Silver

*Color shown as AquaCreme/AquaColor mix.

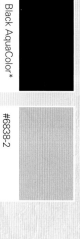

#6883-1

Black AquaColor*

#6838-2

ME 150

tip

This technique can be done over any painted wall color. Always use a drywall mud/paint mix of a different color so that you can see how much texture is added to the wall.

1 Basecoat

Basecoat the wall with White Wheat. Let dry 24 hours.

2 Make drywall mud/paint mix

Make a drywall mud/paint mix (see page 10) using Antique Cream. Trowel on thick and thin areas, leaving open spaces. The thick areas will dry and create a crackled finish. Let dry overnight.

Faux Metal

4 Apply glaze/paint mix

Make a mix of ½-cup (8cl) Black AquaColor to one cup of AquaCreme (24cl)—or one part black latex paint to three parts AquaGlaze. Roll the black mix onto the wall. Then use the chip brush to scrub the mix into the nooks and crannies.

3 Apply silver paint

Use Modern Masters Silver to basecoat the walls. Apply two coats. Let dry one hour between coats.

5 Soften glaze

See "How to Glaze" on page 11. However, there is no need to mist the walls with water.

goldy rocks

Warm and buttery—these are the kinds of colors that soothe the soul. AquaStone, from Faux Effects, is used to create this beautiful "stone" wall. This is a perfect finish for kitchens that need texture instead of color. Because of its warm color and unique texture, this wall treatment looks great with either wood or painted cabinets.

tip

Expect to use a lot of chip brushes, because the bristles will wear down.

Supplies

- Paint rollers and pans
- AquaStone
- Latex gloves
- Sea sponge
- Metal or plastic trowel
- Spray bottle with water
- AquaGlaze
- 3-inch (76mm) chip brushes
- Terry cloth towels
- Porter Paint #6842-1
  Antique Ivory (satin)
- Modern Masters Metallic
  ME 200 Pale Gold

#6842-1

ME200*

* Color shown as glaze/paint mix.

1 Basecoat

Basecoat the walls with Antique
Ivory. Let dry 24 hours.

2 Apply AquaStone

Make sure to use gloves when applying
AquaStone. Use a wet sea sponge, and
apply thicker in some areas and thinner
in other areas. Be sure to leave some
open spaces.

3 Knock down peaks

When the AquaStone has set a minute but is still wet, use a trowel to lightly knock down any peaks. Hold your trowel parallel to the wall. Let dry overnight.

4 Apply glaze/paint mix

Make up the glaze/paint mix (see page 11), using Modern Masters Pale Gold. For easier glazing, mist the wall with water before applying the glaze/paint mix. Use a 3-inch (76mm) chip brush and scrub the glaze/paint mix into the wall.

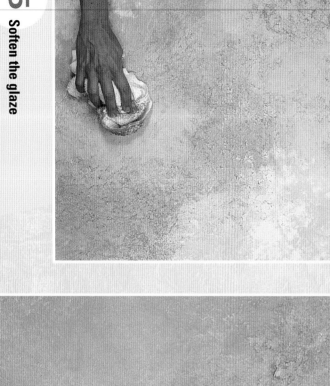

5 Soften the glaze

Then take a dry terry cloth towel and pounce all over the area just glazed to remove the excess glaze and to soften and blend.

Goldy Rocks

have a nice
day striae

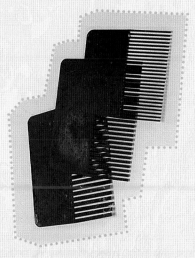

If you're not familiar with this technique, you're probably not familiar with the pronunciation. "Striae" has a long "i," a long "a" and a silent "e." To striae is to create lines or stripes of texture on a surface. You'll surely have a nice day when the results of this striae make your room sing. This finish is so easy and forgiving! You'll have no problem with the technique, and the transformation will be magical.

Supplies

- Paint roller and pan
- Golden Gel Medium, High Solid Gel (Gloss)
- Buckets or other containers
- Venetian trowel
- Metal or plastic trowel
- Metal comb
- AquaGlaze
- 3-inch (76mm) chip brushes
- terry cloth towels
- Porter Paint #6908-1 Irish Linen (satin)
- Porter Paint #6935-3 Prairie Sumac (satin)

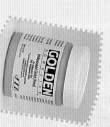

#6908-1

#6935-3*

* Color shown as glaze/paint mix.

1 Basecoat

Basecoat the wall with Irish Linen. Let dry for 24 hours.

2 Apply paint/gel medium mix

Make a mix of equal parts paint (Irish Linen) and gel medium. It should be the consistency of pudding. Trowel onto the wall, working in 2' x 4' (.5m x 1m) sections.

3 Comb through the surface

Take a comb and randomly pull it up and down through the paint/gel medium surface. The gel medium stays wet long enough for you to comb back into your last combed section, but, as with any faux finish, you need to work quickly. Let dry overnight.

Have a Nice Day Striae

4 Apply glaze/paint mix

Mix two parts AquaGlaze to one part Prairie Sumac. Work in 2' x 4' (.5m x 1m) sections and use your chip brush to brush the glaze mix in the same direction as the striae. Make sure to get the glaze mix into all the nooks and crannies on the wall.

5 Soften the glaze

Working in the same direction as the striae, wipe off the excess glaze with a dry terry cloth towel.

sand
castle walls

Here's your chance to go back to your childhood sandbox. Grab a few handfuls of sand and have fun! You'll be surprised at the amazing wall texture you can create with such a simple ingredient. And the glaze mix you apply will give your walls lustrous shine.

Supplies

- Paint roller and pan
- Golden Gel Medium, High Solid Gel (Gloss)
- 2 trowels
- 2 drywall blades
- All-purpose sand
- AquaGlaze
- 3-inch (76mm) chip brushes
- Terry cloth towels
- Porter Paint #6908-1 Irish Linen (satin)
- Porter Paint #6689-4 Deep Dosinia (satin)

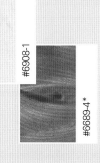

#6908-1

#6689-4*

* Color shown as glaze/paint mix.

1 See previous technique

Basecoat walls with Irish Linen. Follow steps 1 and 2 of "Have a Nice Day Striae" on page 30.

2 Apply sand mixture

In a separate container, mix one part sand to five parts paint/gel medium mix (add more sand if you want a thicker, more grainy texture). Using a separate trowel and drywall blade, spread sand mixture onto the wall in random areas. Make some sand areas thicker than others. Keep your paint/gel and sand mixture application trowels separate and clean! Let dry overnight.

4 Soften the glaze

Take a dry terry cloth towel to remove the excess glaze, blending and softening. Work in a 2' x 3' (.5m x1m) section at a time. Follow the "How to Glaze" directions on page 11.

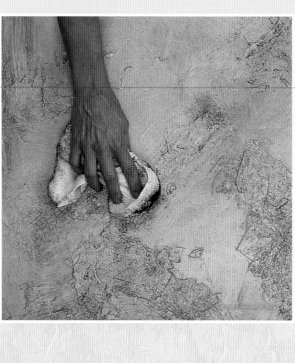

3 Apply glaze/paint mix

Make a mix of two parts AquaGlaze to one part paint (Deep Dosinia). Use a roller to apply to the walls. Use a 3-inch (76mm) chip brush to scrub the glaze mix into all the nooks and crannies.

Sand Castle Walls

floating gems

Put a little sparkle into your life with these simple yet interesting floating gems added directly to your textured wall. You can coordinate any colors found in fabrics and artwork with this technique.

Supplies

- Paint roller and pan
- Rapid-Bond Lite 90 Setting Type Joint Compound powder
- Drill and mixing attachment
- Buckets and other containers
- Venetian trowel
- Metal or plastic trowel
- Terry cloth towels
- Spray bottle with water
- AquaGlaze
- Assorted gems
- 3-inch (76mm) chip brushes
- Porter Paint #6838-2 Antique Cream (satin)
- Porter Paint #6774-4 Muted Copper (satin)

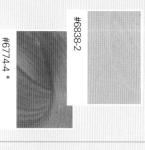

#6838-2

#6774-4 *

*Color shown as glaze/paint mix.

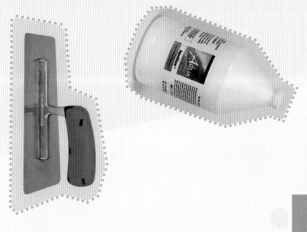

1 Basecoat and apply mud/paint mix

Basecoat walls with Antique Cream. Let dry 24 hours. Make a drywall mud/paint mix (see page 10) with the Antique Cream. Trowel the mud/paint mix on the wall. You can create as much or as little texture as you'd like. Thicker areas can crack—this creates an "Old World" finish. Let dry completely.

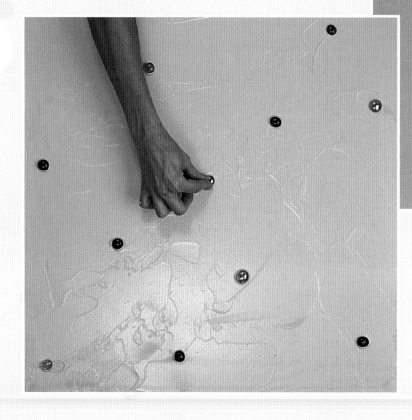

2 Apply Gems

While the plaster is still wet, stick the gems onto the wall in a random pattern. Press and twist each gem into the plaster to make sure it adheres. Let dry completely. Don't worry about the drywall/paint mix getting on your gems. When dry, the mix will scrape off with your fingernail.

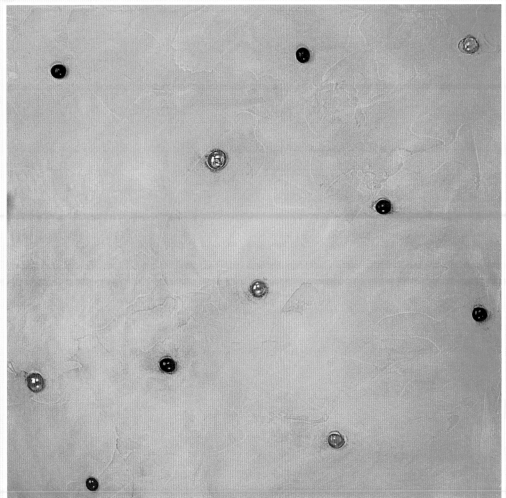

3 Apply glaze/paint mix

Make up your glaze/paint mix (see page 11) with Muted Copper. Use a 3-inch (76mm) chip brush to apply the glaze, making sure to get the glaze into all the nooks and crannies on the wall. The glaze will naturally collect around the gems, which will enhance the look.

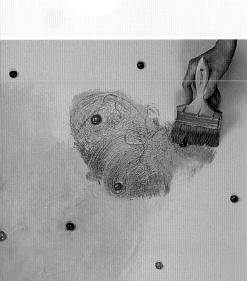

4 Soften the glaze

Take a damp terry cloth towel and rub the glaze into the wall texture. Use a dry terry cloth towel to soften and blend. Follow the "How to Glaze" directions on page 11. Also wipe any excess glaze off the gems.

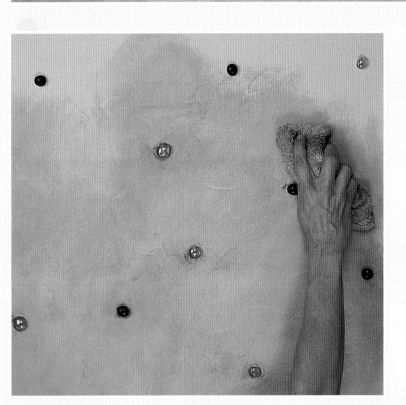

gems

Floating Gems

37

scrolls & jewels

Inspired by the work of Margaret Mackintosh and Gustav Klimt, this technique has been a favorite of mine for years. The movement, the "jewels" and the shimmer on the walls give me a feeling of softness and freedom.

This treatment can be either formal or fun, depending on how much scrolling and embellishing you add. I have scrolled my way around town with this one!

tip

Be creative and use different colored gems to contrast and coordinate with the room décor.

Ambience Salon Spa by The Hairy Cactus

Supplies

- Paint roller and pan
- Rapid-Bond Lite 90 Setting Type Joint Compound powder
- Drill and mixing attachment
- Buckets or other containers
- Venetian trowel
- Metal or plastic trowel
- Screwdriver
- Flat-back marble gems
- AquaGlaze
- 3-inch (76mm) chip brushes
- Spray bottle and water
- Terry cloth towels
- Cotton t-shirt rags
- Artist brush
- Porter Paint #6933-2 Ripe Riesling (satin)
- Porter Paint #6396-3 Deep Peacock (satin)
- Porter Paint #6935-3 Prairie Sumac (satin)
- Modern Masters Metallic ME 661 Tequila Gold

#6935-3**

ME 661**

#6933-2*

#6396-3**

*Color shown as drywall mud/paint mix.

**Color shown as glaze/paint mix.

1 Basecoat, mix mud/paint mix

Basecoat the walls with Porter Paint Ripe Riesling. Let dry for 24 hours. Make up the drywall mud/paint mix (see page 10) with Ripe Riesling. Test the drywall mud thickness by putting some onto the trowel and seeing if a gem sticks without sliding. On the other hand, make sure your mud isn't too thick, or it will set up too fast and be hard to work with.

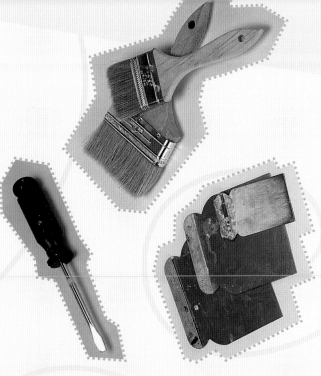

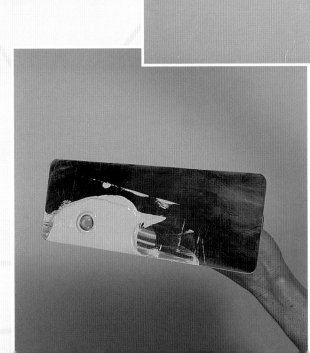

2 Apply drywall mud/paint mix

Work in a 2' x 3' (.5m x 1m) area. Trowel on a medium-thick layer of drywall mud/paint mix, cleaning your trowel as you go. Make sure you get full coverage in each area.

3 "Draw" scrolls & leaves

While the drywall mud/paint mix is still wet, draw connecting random scrolls and leaves into the mud/paint mix with a screwdriver. There will be some material left on the screwdriver after you draw each scroll. Take some of this material and place it on the end of the scroll, making sure to wipe the excess off the screwdriver.

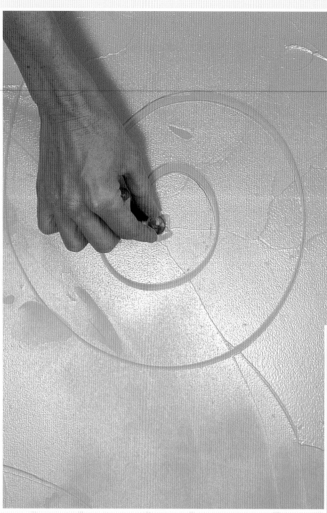

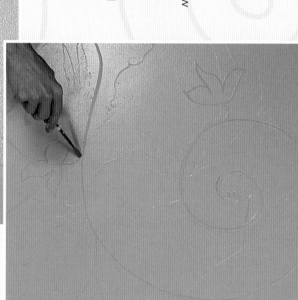

tip

If your glaze/paint mix starts to dry too quickly, spritz the wall with a water bottle to dampen the surface. Be fluid—not stiff.

4 Place gems

Place a gem into the material at the end of the scroll. Press and twist the gem into the drywall. Move on to the next section of wall and repeat steps 3 and 4. Let dry overnight.

5 Apply glaze/paint mix

Create a mix of 3 parts AquaGlaze with 1 part paint color for each of the Porter Paint colors. Using the same brush, apply each glaze/paint color randomly over the wall. Scrub the color around the jewels and into the scrolls (see "How to Glaze" on page 11).

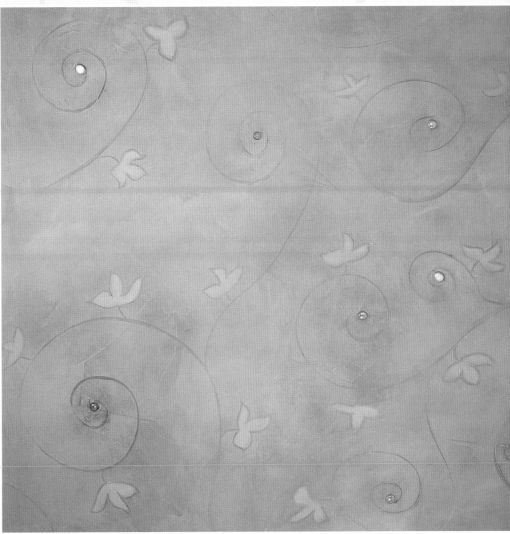

6 Remove excess glaze

As you work each section, make sure to wipe out the leaves. To do this, wrap a wet cotton t-shirt rag around your finger and wipe the color off of the leaves so that they return to their original background color. Clean any glaze/paint off the wall jewels.

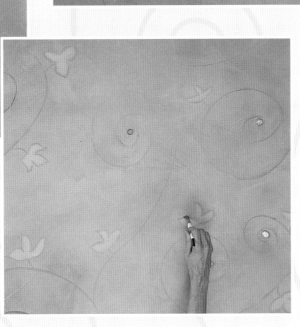

7 Paint in additional color

After the wall has dried, use an artist brush to paint in the carved grooves of the scrolls and leaves with a Tequila Gold glaze/paint mix. Keep a wet rag handy to wipe off any excess glaze/paint that gets outside the grooves.

Scrolls & Jewels

lucky charms

I "lucked" into this design because my "Lucky Charms" client, internationally syndicated cartoonist, Jim Borgman, has a playful, witty personality. He loved "Scrolls & Jewels," but didn't feel it had enough whimsy for him. "Instead of leaves, make hearts, moons and stars," he said. "Make it bright and cheerful, because this is my work environment!"

As you can see, it's spectacular.

Home of Jim Borgman & Suzanne Soled

Supplies

- Paint roller and pan
- Venetian trowel
- Metal or plastic trowel
- Rapid-Bond Lite 90 Setting Type Joint Compound powder
- Drill and mixing attachment
- Buckets or other containers
- Screwdriver
- Flat-back marble gems in various colors
- AquaGlaze
- 3-inch (76mm) chip brushes
- Spray bottle with water
- Terry cloth towels
- Cotton t-shirt rag
- Artist brush
- Porter Paint #6933-2 Ripe Riesling (satin)
- Porter Paint #6267-3 Lime Juice (satin)
- Porter Paint #6396-3 Deep Peacock (satin)
- Porter Paint #6930-3 Bayou Bronze (satin)
- Modern Masters Metallic ME 247 Sage

#6396-3**

#6267-3*

#6930-3**

#6933-2**

#ME 247**

*Color shown as dry-wall mud/paint mix.
**Color shown as glaze/paint mix.

Follow all the steps for "Scrolls & Jewels" on pages 39 through 41 with these adjustments: (1) Use Lime Juice paint color for the basecoat and the mud/paint mix. (2) Instead of carving leaves into the drywall mud/paint mix, use a screwdriver to carve hearts, moons and stars. (3) Use the paint colors in the supply list to the right for the glaze/paint mixtures.

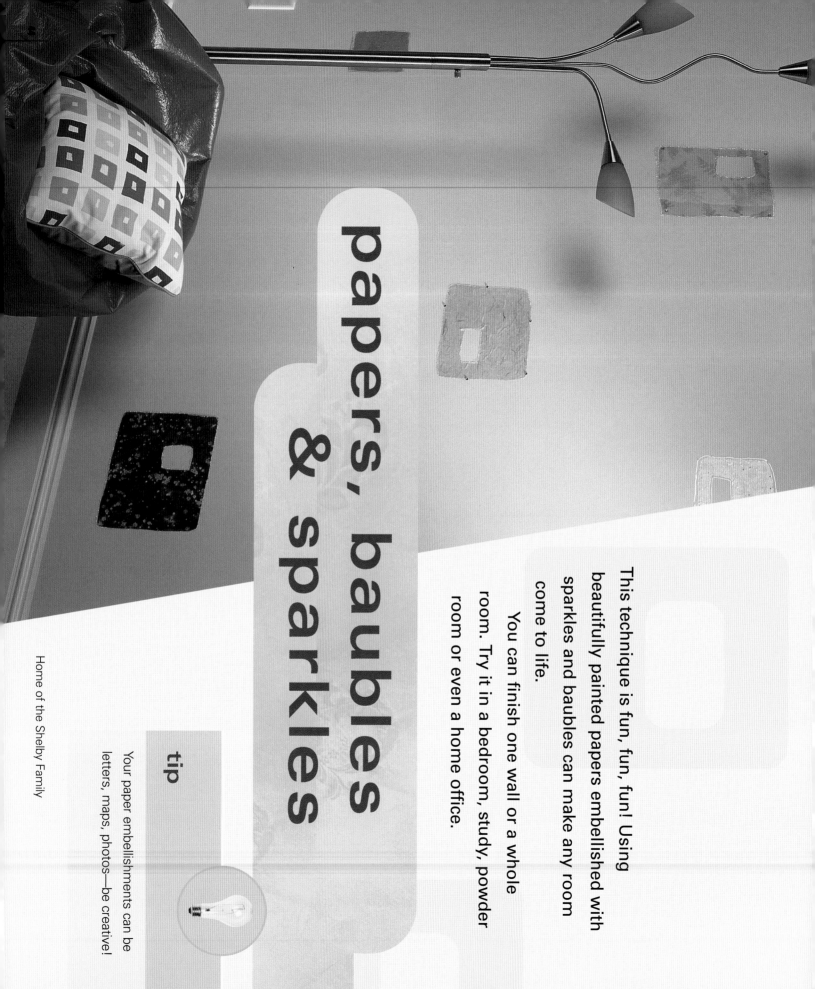

papers, baubles & sparkles

This technique is fun, fun, fun! Using beautifully painted papers embellished with sparkles and baubles can make any room come to life.

You can finish one wall or a whole room. Try it in a bedroom, study, powder room or even a home office.

tip

Your paper embellishments can be letters, maps, photos—be creative!

Supplies

- Paint roller and pan
- Assorted decorative papers (scrapbook papers, wallpapers, etc.)
- Scissors
- Wallpaper paste (heavy duty clear)
- Chip brushes (Select sizes appropriate for applying paste to your decorative papers.)
- Rags
- Bucket of water
- Glitter glue
- 3-D paints
- Assorted flat-back gems
- YES! paste
- 3M Safe-Release tape
- Porter Paint #6404-1 China Blue (satin)

#6704-1

1 Basecoat

Basecoat the wall with China Blue paint. Allow 24 hours to dry.

2 Cut & apply paste to decorative paper

Take the decorative paper and cut out rectangular and square shapes. Make the cut-outs all different sizes, and keep both the inner shapes and outer portions of your cut papers, because you'll use them both. Use your chip brush to apply clear wallpaper paste onto the back of each sheet of paper. Make sure you apply a generous layer of paste and get full coverage on the back of the paper. Be careful to keep your work surface clean of all wall-paper paste!

3 Apply papers

Randomly place the squares on the wall so that there is a nice balance. Make sure the papers are level. Press down with a dry rag. Remove and clean any excess wallpaper paste with a wet rag, being careful not to get the paper wet, as the paper will bubble. Place a variety of different paper designs around each other. Allow papers to dry on the wall for 24 hours before moving on to the next step.

4 Outline paper edges

Outline all the paper edges with glitter glue or 3-D paints in colors that contrast and coordinate with the papers. Be creative with your glitter glue and paint—you don't necessarily have to stay on the lines or use the same color all over each paper. Just use your imagination.

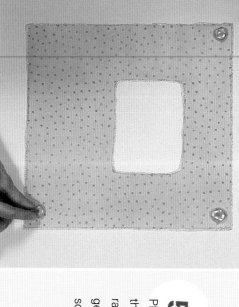

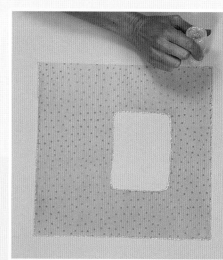

5 Apply gems

Place smaller gems into the wet glue or paint at random. Adhere some gems around the squares with YES! paste.

tip

Make sure the rag you use is only lightly dampened. If it's too wet, the papers will bubble.

6 Keep gems in place

Make sure the heavier gems stay in place until the YES! paste dries by using 3M Safe-Release tape to secure them. Use long strips of tape and be careful not to touch the tape to the wet glue, 3-D paint or papers.

Papers, Baubles & Sparkles

My super-creative designer said, "I want pink scrolls on orange walls, and orange scrolls on pink!" "Cool," I said, "but can I add sparkles?" "Of course," she said. "Make it all aglitter!"

Don't be afraid to choose your own fun color combinations to reflect your personal taste and style!

it's all aglitter

Home of the Shelby Family

Supplies

- Paint rollers and pans
- 3M Safe-Release tape
- Level
- Artist brush (See step 2.)
- 1-inch (25mm) flat artist brush
- Ultra-fine glitter (pink & orange color)
- YES! paste
- Chip brush
- Porter Paint #6113-5 Chinese Lantern (satin)
- Porter Paint #6071-6 Brite Fuschia (satin)

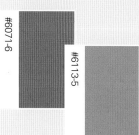

#6071-6

#6113-5

1 Basecoat

Divide your wall into thirds. The top third of the wall is painted with Chinese Lantern. The bottom two-thirds is painted with Brite Fuschia. Make sure you tape off the wall perfectly, using 3M Safe-Release tape and a level.

2 Paint scrolls

Using an artist brush of a size you're comfortable with, paint your scrolls on the wall. Use the paint color that is the opposite of the wall color. For an interesting effect, plan on letting some scrolls extend into the lower wall color. (You'll paint the portion of the scroll on the lower color in the next step.)

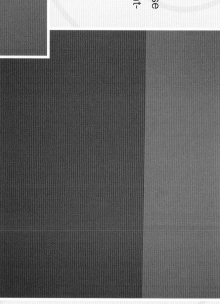

3 Use fluid movements

When you paint the scrolls in the lower area, first finish the scrolls that began in the upper area. Then paint scrolls extending from those lower portions. Keep your movements fluid. Let the paint dry overnight.

It's All Aglitter

tip

If you are not comfortable painting your scrolls freehand, draw them with chalk first. Be fluid!

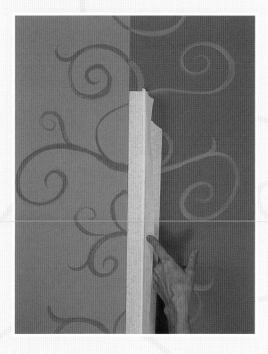

4 Make a trough

Make a trough to catch loose sparkles. Take two pieces of 2-inch (51mm) wide 3M Safe-Release tape. Overlap the edges of the two pieces, and adhere them under the area where you're working. Lift the lower piece of tape up and make a fold. Take a third piece of tape and place it along the outside of the fold. You may need to angle smaller pieces of tape at the trough ends to keep them from falling under the weight of the glitter.

5 Paint & glitter scrolls

Using the artist brush and the YES! paste, paint over the scrolls. Do one scroll at a time before the paste dries. Place the pink ultra-fine glitter into a container that you can place your brush in. Take a 1-inch (25mm) soft, flat brush, scoop the sparkles onto the brush and brush over the paste-covered scroll. The trough will catch any loose or extra sparkles. Wipe away any loose sparkles on the wall with a clean chip brush. Repeat the process with the lower scrolls, using orange ultra-fine glitter.

embellished butterflies

I believe that a girl can't have enough sparkly butterflies in her room. With this finish you can really go for it! Add anything that sparkles—check out your local craft or scrapbooking store or antique mall for things that glitter. Use pearls, jewels, squeeze paint and more! Experiment and express yourself to personalize your room.

Supplies

- Laser Excel butterfly stencil
- 3M Safe-Release tape
- Small trowel
- YES! paste
- 1-inch (25mm) soft bristle artist brush
- Ultra-fine glitter
- Assorted jewels, craft paint, glitter squeeze paint, etc.
- Chip brush

Embellished Butterflies

1 Complete the wall surface (no photo)

The butterflies can be done on a painted or glazed wall. Complete your wall surface first and let dry.

2 Stencil

Tape the stencil to the wall. Use a small trowel with YES! paste and trowel through the butterfly stencil.

3 Apply glitter

Make a trough (see page 49) to catch extra sparkle glitter. Apply the glitter onto the area where the YES! paste has been applied, using the soft bristle artist brush. Using your creativity, add jewels, craft paint, etc. to embellish the butterflies. After everything has dried overnight, take a chip brush and brush away any excess glitter, etc.

gift wrap

I have some very creative clients. Sometimes they even like to join me in a project at their homes. Such was the case with the "Gift Wrap" wall. We had a blast doing this project together. It all started because I can't tie a bow worth a darn. My client, Nancy, volunteered, and the next thing I knew, she made all the bows on the wall. I still haven't learned how to tie a proper bow!

take note

Paint color and paper used in the step-by-step demonstrations are different from the wall photo on this page.

Home of Nancy Williams

1 Basecoat & size the wall

Basecoat the wall with Lime Juice. Let dry 24 hours. Size the walls with wallpaper sizing.

2 Measure the wall

Measure the wall to find the midpoint. Mark the midpoint and make a vertical plum line (make sure the line is faint).

3 Adhere decorative paper to the wall

Take a piece of decorative paper and fold it in half to find the middle. Mark the middle with chalk or tape. Apply wallpaper paste to the back of the decorative paper. Make sure the paper is completely pasted. Using the chalk/tape on the paper as your guide, place the marks at the plumb line and adhere the paper to the wall at the ceiling.

Supplies

- Paint roller and pan
- Wallpaper sizing
- Plumb
- Decorative papers
- Wallpaper paste
- Scissors
- Level
- Decorative ribbons
- Staple gun and staples
- Porter Paint #6267-3 Lime Juice (satin)

#6267-3

tip

Instead of tying bows in the center where the ribbons cross, you can attach a tassel or silk flower—anything you love or that expresses your personality.

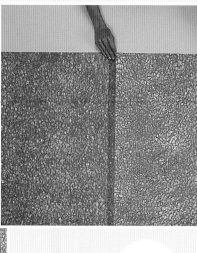

4 Apply second paper piece

When applying the next piece of paper, make sure to overlap the seams about 1 inch (3cm). Do the whole middle column, starting at the ceiling and working towards the bottom.

5 Cover the wall

Cover the wall completely with decorative paper, checking with your level along the way.

6 Attach ribbon

Staple your ribbon to the wall, starting at the first seam in the furthest corner. Fold your raw edge under, make the edge flush with the wall and then staple the end to the wall. Stretch your ribbon across at a diagonal to the opposite bottom seam.

7 Attach bows

After you have finished stapling the ribbon to the wall, take complementary ribbon and tie it in a bow where the wall ribbons cross.

Gift Wrap

I had all this extra fringe, so I thought, "Why not?!" I glued it to the wall. Wow! What an impact!

See what you can do when you use ordinary products in unexpected ways. This look is so unique—you have to try it.

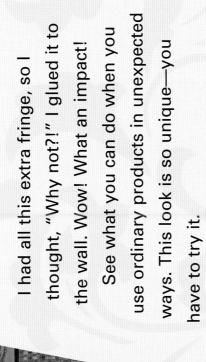

fringe benefits

Supplies

- Rapid-Bond Lite 90 Setting Type Joint Compound powder
- Drill and mixing attachment
- Buckets or other containers
- Venetian trowel
- Metal or plastic trowel
- AquaGlaze
- Paint roller and pan
- Terry cloth towels
- Spray bottle with water
- Royal Design Studio stencil #524 Scrollallover
- Pencil
- Level
- 3-inch (76mm) chip brushes
- 2 Japan scrapers
- 3M Safe-Release tape
- FolkArt Berry Wine acrylic paint
- Stencil brush
- YES! paste
- Any decorative fringe attached to a ribbon trim
- Velvet or decorative ribbon
- Heavy-duty staple gun and staples
- Porter Paint #6842-1 Antique Ivory (satin)
- Porter Paint #6838-2 Antique Cream (satin)
- Porter Paint #6761-2 Post Oak (satin)

#6838-2

#6842-1

#6761-2*

*Color shown as glaze/paint mix.

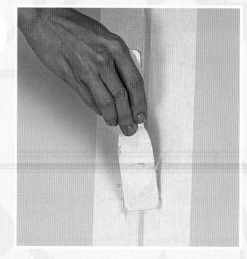

1 Apply wall treatment

Base your wall with Antique Ivory. Tape off the top third of your wall from the bottom two-thirds with the Safe Release tape. For the bottom two-thirds of the wall, follow the "Fresco Style in a Little While" instructions, found on page 19, using Antique Cream. The top third is finished with the "Royal Relief" technique found on pages 84 through 85. The stencil used in this technique is from Royal Design Studio, #524 Scrollallover. Again, use the drywall mud/Antique Cream paint mix, troweled through the stencil. The wall glaze color is AquaGlaze mixed with Post Oak. After the glaze has dried, take the Scrollallover stencil and lay it back over the stenciled wall. Using a stencil brush, rub in a circular motion and color the stencil in with Post Oak glaze and a touch of FolkArt Berry Wine acrylic paint. Let dry for 24 hours.

2 Prepare wall for fringe trim

Put two pieces of Safe Release tape on the wall, leaving ¼-inch (6mm) of wall showing through. Take a thin trowel with YES! paste and trowel a generous layer of the paste on the ¼-inch (6mm) wall space.

tip

You can put YES! paste into a cake decorating bag. Use Wilton cake decorating tip #5, and squeeze the glue onto the ribbon part of the fringe.

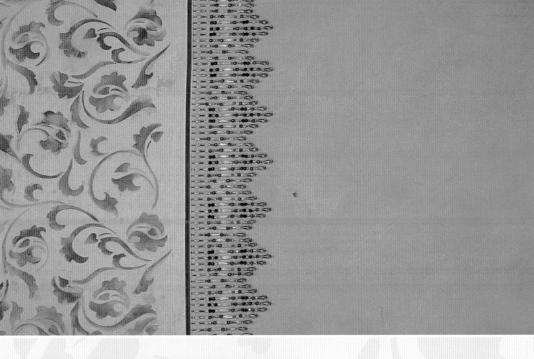

3 Apply fringe

Remove the tape. Apply the fringe by pressing the ribbon part of the fringe to the pasted area. Staple as you go, approximately every 4 to 6 inches (10 to 15cm). Make sure the back side of the fringe tape is glued and stapled to the wall, so that the fringe hangs correctly.

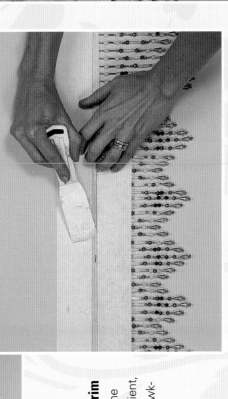

4 Apply glue for ribbon trim

Repeat step 2 over the top of the ribbon part of the fringe. Be patient, masking off the fringe can be awkward. Just move slowly.

5 Apply ribbon trim

Remove the tape and place the velvet ribbon over the glued area and over the fringe.

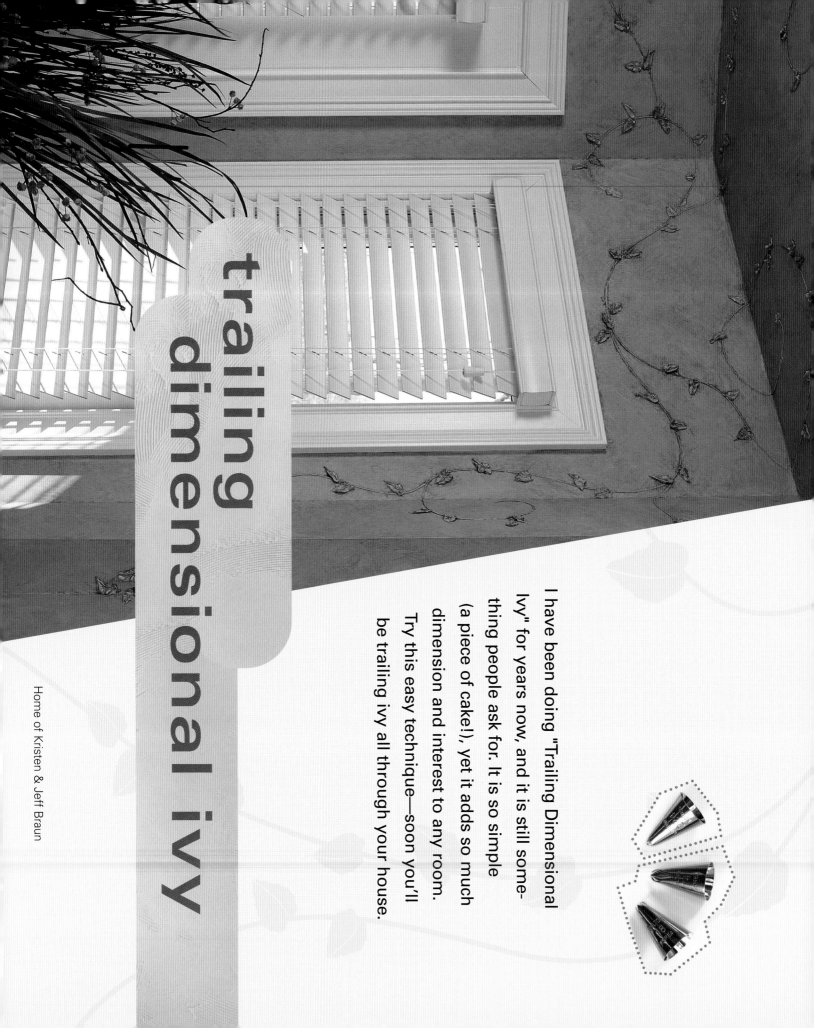

trailing dimensional ivy

Home of Kristen & Jeff Braun

I have been doing "Trailing Dimensional Ivy" for years now, and it is still something people ask for. It is so simple (a piece of cake!), yet it adds so much dimension and interest to any room. Try this easy technique—soon you'll be trailing ivy all through your house.

---

piece of cake

Supplies

- Liquitex Modeling Paste
- Cake decorating bags (regular size)
- Wilton cake decorating tips #5 (for vine), #70 (for leaves)
- Coupler (keeps the tips on the bag)
- Paint stirring stick
- AquaGlaze
- 3-inch (76mm) chip brushes
- Terry cloth towels
- Porter Paint #6838-2 Antique Cream (satin)
- Porter Paint #6761-2 Post Oak (satin)
- Porter Paint #6798-3 Red Earth (satin)

#6838-2

#6798-3*

#6761-2*

*Color swatch shown as glaze/paint mix.

tip

Before applying the trailing ivy to a wall, practice on another surface to get comfortable. Strive for a continuous, fluid movement.

1 Basecoat

Basecoat the walls with Antique Cream. Let dry 24 hours.

2 Apply vine to wall

Place the modeling paste into the cake decorating bags. Use the #5 tip for creating the vines. Use a paint stirring stick to scoop the paste into the bag. Always keep the lid on the paste when it's not in use, so that the paste doesn't dry up. Trail the vine randomly around windows and doors, with a continuous, fluid motion.

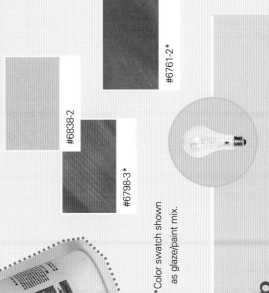

59

3 Apply the leaves

Rinse out the used tip right away! Then switch to the #70 tip to create leaves. Add leaves in a decorative yet random fashion. Make sure to wipe the tip off between leaves. If the leaf splits when you are making it, don't worry. This gives an antique, Old World look. Let dry overnight before continuing with the next step.

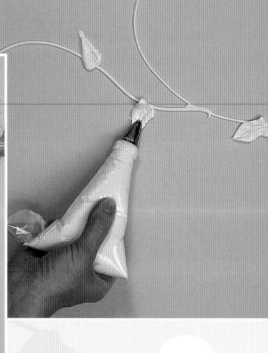

If you are not happy with the placement of a vine or leaf, wipe it off with a wet rag before it hardens.

4 Glaze the walls

Make up your glaze/paint mixes (see page 11), one for Post Oak and one for Red Earth. Use your chip brush and randomly use a circular motion to rub each color into the ivy, making sure to get the glaze/paint mix into all the nooks and crannies. On other areas of the wall, just spread the glaze/paint mixes randomly.

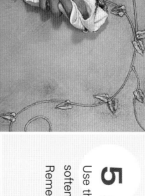

5 Soften the color

Use the terry cloth rag to blend and soften the color all over the wall. Remember to feather out your edges.

Trailing Dimensional Ivy

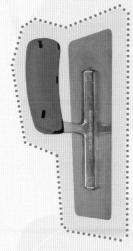

In this project, the grapes and leaves are created with drywall mud. Grapes are a classic motif—they never go out of style. Whether you create a mural, stencil or embellish your walls with 3-D grapes and leaves, there is something about Tuscan motifs that attracts everyone. The beauty, the romance, the history, the music...ahhh! Who wouldn't want a little bit of Italy in their home?

napa valley 1

Home of the Wolf Family

Supplies

- Paint roller and pan
- Rapid-Bond Lite 90 Setting Type Joint Compound powder
- Drill and mixing attachment
- Buckets or other containers
- Venetian trowel
- Metal or plastic trowel
- Liquitex Modeling Paste
- Cake decorating bags
- Wilton cake decorating tip #5 (vine), #70 (leaves), #12 (grapes)
- Coupler (keeps the tips on the bag)
- Paint stirring stick
- Grape leaf stencil (in various sizes)
- 3M Safe-Release tape
- Screwdriver
- AquaGlaze
- 3-inch (76mm) chip brushes
- Terry cloth towels
- Artist brush
- Blender/extender
- Burnt Carmine acrylic craft paint
- Olive green acrylic craft paint
- Brown acrylic craft paint
- YES! paste (if needed)
- Porter Paint #6896-1 Off White (satin)
- Porter Paint #6694-3 Dover Beige (satin)

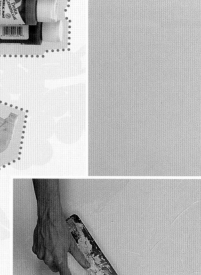

#6896-1 *

#6694-3 **

*Color shown as drywall mud/paint mix

**Color shown as glaze/paint mix

tip

Use two cake decorator bags, one inside the other, when making grapes. One bag by itself is not very strong, but when doubled up, they should last longer.

1 Basecoat & apply drywall mud/paint mix

Basecoat the wall with Off White. Let dry 24 hours. Then make a drywall mud/Off White paint mix (see page 10) and trowel a texture onto the wall. Let dry overnight. Lay out your design by following steps 2 and 3 of "Trailing Dimensional Ivy" (see pages 59–60). Let dry.

2 Create grapes

Make up a mix of 1½–2 cups (35–47cl) drywall mud to 10–12 ounces (30–35cl) of paint. The mixture will have the consistency of peanut butter. Scoop some drywall mud/paint mix into the cake decorator bag. Using tip #12, lay out one cluster of grapes onto the wall (they will have little "tails," which you can push to the side). Make sure the grapes are fairly plump, as they will shrink when dry. After you've created your basic bunch of grapes, place another layer randomly over the base layer to add dimension.

3 Create leaves

After the grape clusters have dried, tape your grape leaf stencil to the wall in various places around the clusters. Using the same texture that you applied to the wall, trowel the mud/paint mix through the stencil.

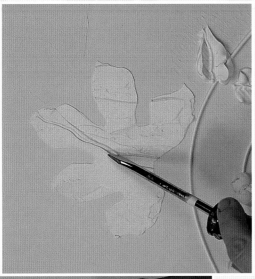

4 Leaf veins

While the leaves are wet, take a screwdriver and etch in leaf veins. Look at a natural leaf for guidance—no squiggly, snakey veins!

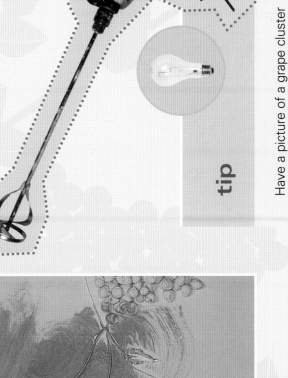

tip

Have a picture of a grape cluster on hand as you're working to help you make your clusters look realistic.

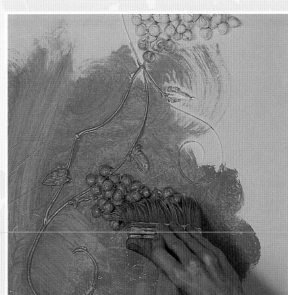

5 Connect stems to leaves

Change to a #5 tip on your cake decorator bag and make stems to connect the leaves and the grapes. Let dry thoroughly—up to three days—before moving on to the next step.

6 Apply glaze

Make a glaze/paint mix with Dover Beige (see page 11). Use a 3-inch (76mm) chip brush with a circular motion and scrub the glaze/paint mix into the grapes and vines. Make sure to get into all the nooks and crannies. Use a roller to roll on the glaze/paint mix over the rest of the wall (see page 11).

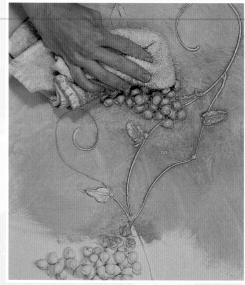

7 Soften glaze

Take a terry cloth towel to soften and remove the excess glaze/paint mix. Let dry.

8 Paint the vines, stems & leaves

Use an artist brush to paint the vine and the stems with a brown acrylic paint that has extender added for easier application. Paint the leaves, using olive green acrylic paint and added extender. Vary the color intensity of the leaves so that they don't all look the same.

tip

If any grapes fall off the wall while you're painting or glazing, glue them back with YES! paste.

9 Paint the grapes

Paint the grapes with a soft bristle artist brush, using Burnt Carmine and a bit of blender/extender. Make sure you get into all the nooks and crannies between each grape. Take a damp rag and occasionally wipe off a bit of paint to simulate a highlighted spot.

napa valley 2

In this project, the grapes are faux "gems."

#6838-2

ME 200*

*Color shown as glaze/paint mix

Supplies

- AquaGlaze
- Paint roller and pan
- Liquitex Modeling Paste
- Cake decorating bags
- Wilton cake decorating tips #5 (vine), #70 (leaves)
- Coupler (keeps tips on the bag)
- Paint stirring stick
- Artist brush
- Olive green acrylic craft paint
- Brown acrylic craft paint
- Marble Accents red gems
- YES! paste
- 3M Safe-Release tape
- Polymer clay
- Grape leaf stencil
- Scissors
- Glass baking dish
- Porter Paint #6838-2 Antique Cream
- Modern Masters Metallic ME 200 Pale Gold

1 Base wall & apply the finish

Basecoat the walls with Antique Cream. Let dry 24 hours. Finish the walls with a soft blending of Modern Masters Pale Gold (one part) and AquaGlaze (three parts). Let dry for 24 hours. Then apply the vine and leaves per directions in "Trailing Dimensional Ivy," pages 59-60. When dry, paint the vine with brown paint and extender.

2 Create grape clusters

Use Marble Accents red gems and glue on the first grape clusters with YES! paste. When the paste has dried, add a few random gems onto the cluster. You will need to secure each layer with tape until dry.

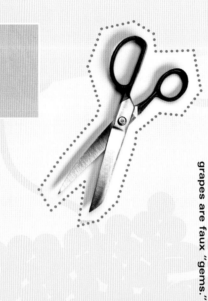

3 Create grape leaves

Make grape leaves out of polymer clay. Flatten out the clay into a ⅛-inch (3mm) pancake. Use a grape leaf stencil as a template and gently press it into the polymer clay, leaving an impression. Cut out the leaf with scissors. Place each leaf into a glass baking pan. Bend and shape some of the leaf edges randomly. Then bake the leaves according to package directions. (Always use a glass pan so that the clay leaves do not burn.)

4 Paint the leaves

After the clay leaves are cool to the touch, paint them with olive green acrylic craft paint. Then use YES! paste to attach them to the wall onto the vine.

napa valley 3

In this project, the grapes and leaves are created with polymer clay.

Supplies

- Paint roller and pan
- AquaStone
- Latex gloves
- Sea sponge
- Trowel
- Liquitex Modeling Paste
- Cake decorating bags
- Wilton cake decorating tip #5 (vine)
- Coupler (keeps the tip on the bag)
- Paint stirring stick
- AquaGlaze
- Chip brush
- Polymer clay
- Grape leaf stencil
- Scissors
- Glass baking dish
- Brown acrylic craft paint
- Olive green acrylic craft paint
- Burnt Carmine acrylic craft paint
- YES! paste
- Porter Paint #6842-1 Antique Ivory (satin)
- Modern Masters Metallic ME 200 Pale Gold

#6842-1

*Color shown as glaze/paint mix

ME 200*

1 Apply the wall finish

Basecoat the wall with Antique Ivory. Let dry 24 hours. Apply AquaStone (see Goldy Rocks, steps 2 and 3, on pages 27-28 for application instructions).

2 Create vines

Create the vines (see "Trailing Dimensional Ivy," step 2, on page 59). Glaze the walls with a mix of AquaGlaze and Modern Masters Pale Gold (see page 11), making sure to glaze the vines first. Roll the rest of the walls with the glaze mixture. Then use a chip brush to blend, soften and remove excess glaze.

3 Create grapes and leaves

Make leaves with polymer clay (see "Napa Valley 2," step 3, on page 66). To make grapes, use polymer clay and roll little balls the size of grapes. About 30-35 balls make one grape cluster. Bake the leaves and grapes in a glass baking dish according to package directions, and then let them cool.

4 Glue and paint leaves and grape clusters

When cool to the touch, affix the grapes and leaves to the wall with YES! paste. For the grape clusters, first glue a base layer of grapes and secure it with tape until the glue dries. Then add a second layer of grapes. Tape again until the glue dries. Then paint the leaves with the olive green craft paint and the grapes with Burnt Carmine craft paint. If you prefer, you can paint the grapes and leaves before you glue them to the wall.

bouquet of roses

Here's another classic motif—who doesn't love a rose! Use this technique for many purposes—to frame a window, to highlight a special room feature or to give a room a garden-like atmosphere. Select paint colors for your roses to complement your décor.

Home of Steve & Sheila Bandy

Supplies

- Paint roller and pans
- Liquitex Modeling Paste
- Cake decorating bags
- Wilton Cake Decorating tip #5 (vine), #70 (leaves)
- Coupler (keeps tips on the bag)
- AquaCreme
- 3-inch (76mm) chip brushes
- Terry cloth towels
- Artist brush
- Medium brown craft paint
- AquaGlaze
- Soft rags
- Polymer clay
- Dental floss
- Glass baking pan
- Light pink acrylic craft paint
- Dark pink acrylic craft paint
- YES! paste
- 3M Safe-Release tape
- AquaBond Off White
- AquaColor Ochre Yellow
- Modern Masters Metallics ME 661 Tequila Gold
- Modern Masters Metallic ME 247 Sage

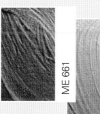

Off White

Ochre Yellow*

ME 661

ME 247*

*Color shown as glaze/paint mix

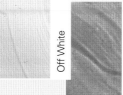

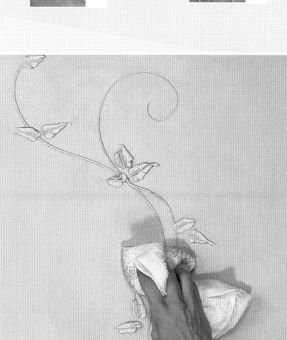

1 Create the wall finish (no photo)

Basecoat the walls with AquaBond Off White. Let dry 24 hours. Follow steps 2 and 3 from "Trailing Dimensional Ivy," pages 59-60.

2 Apply glaze mix into the walls

Make a mix of 30 percent AquaColor Ochre Yellow and 70 percent AquaCreme (about a 1 to 3 ratio). Using a 3-inch (76mm) chip brush, scrub the vine area with a circular motion. Make sure you get into the nooks and crannies of the ivy. Roll AquaColor/AquaCreme mix over the rest of the wall.

3 Soften the glaze

Use a *dry* terry cloth towel or soft rags to soften the mix you just applied. Do not spray with water. Let the glaze dry.

5 Roll the clay into a tube

To make the roses, pinch off a piece of polymer clay, and roll it into a tube shape.

4 Paint the vines & leaves

Using an artist brush, paint the vine with Modern Masters Tequila Gold and a tiny bit of medium brown craft paint; paint the leaves with Modern Masters Sage Green mixed with a small amount of AquaGlaze. Wipe off any excess paint with a damp rag. Don't try to achieve perfection—the vines and leaves look better with some lighter and some darker areas. Let dry.

6 Flatten the clay

Press with your forefingers and thumbs to flatten the clay.

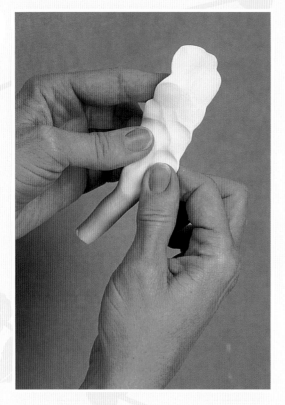

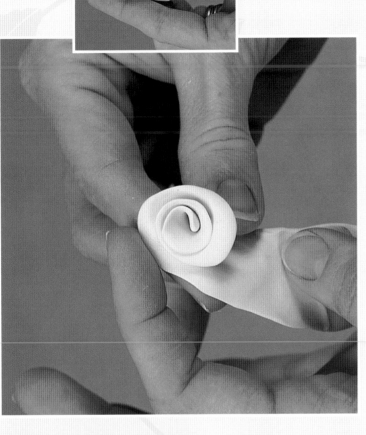

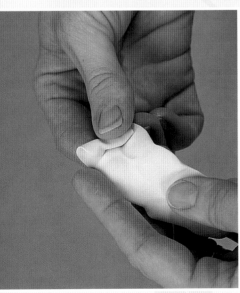

7 Form the roses

Start at one end and roll the clay, pushing the top edges slightly down as you go. Continue rolling, pushing and shaping until you have completed your rose.

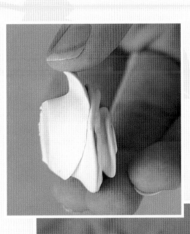

8 Create a flat bottom

Wrap a piece of dental floss around half of the rose bottom and slice. You'll have a flat bottom on your rose. Make all the roses you'll need, place them in a glass baking pan and bake according to the directions on your clay package. Let the roses cool completely.

9 Paint the roses

Paint your roses with light pink and dark pink craft paint before applying them to the wall. First paint the bottom of the rose. Then paint the rose itself, making sure to get into every nook and cranny. Use different paint shades on different parts of the rose to give it dimension and character.

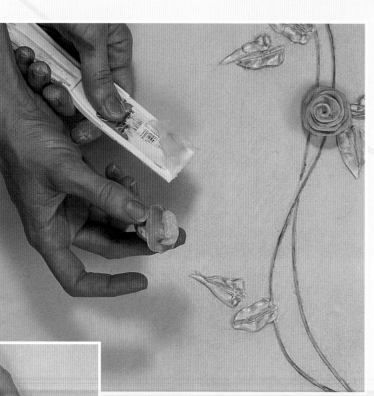

10 Paste the roses on the wall

Apply a generous amount of YES! paste to the back of each rose. Decide where you want to place the rose and attach it firmly to the wall.

tip

When removing the tape, pull slowly so as not to mar your wall finish.

Bouquet of Roses

11 Tape roses in place until dry

Use Safe-Release tape to secure the roses to the wall until the glue is dry.

diamonds in the rough

I was terrible in math, but aced geometry. Now I know why—I have always been attracted to circles, rectangles and diamonds.

You don't need to be a math whiz to apply this technique. Take out your measuring tape or use a template to form the diamond shapes. After that, just paint!

Supplies

- Paint roller and pan
- Tape measure or diamond template
- 3M Safe-Release tape
- Level
- Credit card or other hard plastic edge
- 2-inch (51mm) chip brush
- Porter Paint #6934-2
  Delta Green (satin)
- DecoArt Sandstones DSD21
  Golden Fleck
- AquaColors: Ochre Yellow, Earth
  Brown, Earth Green

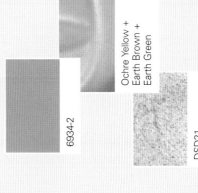

6934-2

Ochre Yellow +
Earth Brown +
Earth Green

DSD21

1 Basecoat

Basecoat the walls with Delta Green.
Allow them to dry for 24 hours.

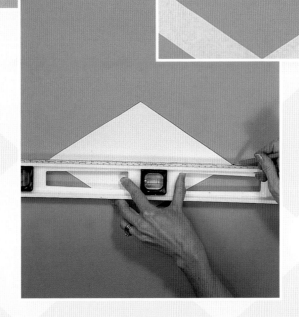

2 Tape off diamond shapes

Use a measuring tape or a
template and a level to
mark your diamond
shapes. Then tape off
your diamonds with 3M
Safe-Release tape.

3 Burnish edges of tape

Burnish the tape edge with a credit card or a piece of hard plastic to seal the edges, so that paint will not seep under the tape.

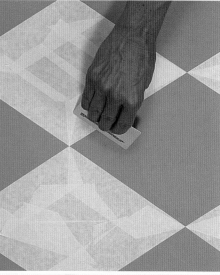

tip

When storing textured paints, place plastic wrap over the paint can or jar, then cover tightly with the lid. This keeps the textured paint fresh for when you want to use it again.

4 Apply the Sandstones

Mix DecoArt Sandstones Golden Fleck tinted with AquaColor Ochre Yellow, Earth Brown and Earth Green. Because Sandstones tints easily, use very small amounts of the AquaColor squirted into the Sandstones. You can also use universal tints to tint the Sandstones. Keep in mind that Sandstones dry approximately 30 percent darker than they appear when wet. Paint this mix onto the exposed diamonds with a 2-inch (51mm) chip brush. Apply the first coat with a generous layer, but be careful not to overwork the Sandstones. Paint one diamond at a time. Let the first coat dry about 4-6 hours or overnight before applying the second coat. Make sure the second coat is applied as generously as the first coat. Allow the diamonds to completely dry before pulling off the tape.

Diamonds in the Rough

buried treasure

I'm always combining one product with another. Sometimes it's a disaster, but most of the time it's an awesome marriage of textures and colors. Faux Effects has a wonderful product called LusterStone. It's beautiful troweled onto a wall by itself or mixed with other products. Here I've troweled Lusterstone through a stencil, sandwiched between two layers of DecoArt Sandstone.

The tone-on-tone look of this technique is perfect in almost any room. You can make the look formal or casual simply by adjusting your choice of colors and stencils.

Supplies

- Paint roller and pan
- Venetian trowel
- Metal or plastic trowel (for scooping material onto Venetian trowel)
- Small trowel (for stenciling)
- Royal Design Studios stencil #700L, Large Florentine
- Porter Paint #7121-3 Hatteras Gray (satin)
- AquaColor Royale Blue
- AquaColor Black
- DecoArt Sandstones DSD21 Golden Fleck
- LusterStone Midnight Blue

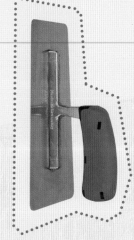

#7121-3

Royale Blue + Black + Golden Fleck

Midnight Blue

1 Basecoat

Basecoat the walls with Hatteras Gray. Let dry 24 hours.

2 Apply Sandstones

Take AquaColors Royale Blue and Black and mix with the DecoArt Sandstones Golden Fleck till you create the desired color. Be careful—Sandstones dries at least 30 percent darker than it appears when wet. Trowel the AquaColor/Sandstones mix onto the wall. Because the material is runny, hold the trowel close to the wall and move the trowel in an upward motion onto the wall. Once the product is on the wall, you can trowel in a normal fashion. Apply a thin, smooth layer (it will drip if applied too thickly). Let dry overnight.

tip

This is a true tone-on-tone look. For more drama, use a contrasting color for your stenciled area.

Buried Treasure

3 Stencil

Tape the stencil onto the wall very securely. Take a small amount of Midnight Blue LusterStone and lightly trowel a thin, smooth layer onto the stencil. Pull off the stencil and let the wall dry overnight.

4 Create the embedded look

Apply the second layer of DecoArt Sandstones Golden Fleck in the same manner as the first, scraping across the LusterStone so the stencil will show through, giving the stencil an embedded look.

simply scrolls

I have a motto—if it's too plain or ugly, add some scrolls or paint it gold! That usually solves the problem. By adding some dimension, color or embellishment, you can change the look and feel of any room.

Make the scrolls big or little—letting the size of your walls be your guide. Create a tone-on-tone finish or use contrasting colors to coordinate with fabrics in the room. Life's too short to be spent with things plain or ugly!

Supplies

- 6-inch (15cm) roller and pan
- Paint stirring stick
- Large, round artist brush
- AquaCreme
- 3-inch (76mm) chip brush
- Terry cloth towels
- AquaSeal
- Porter Paint #6934-2
  Delta Green (satin)
- DecoArt Sandstones DSD21
  Golden Fleck
- AquaColors: Ochre Yellow,
  Earth Brown & Earth Green

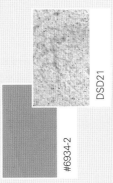

#6934-2

DSD21

Ochre Yellow + Earth
Brown + Earth
Green

1 Basecoat

Basecoat the wall with Delta Green. After the paint is dry, apply one coat of AquaSeal.

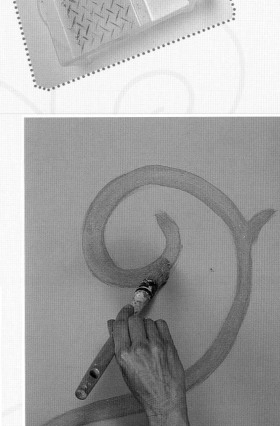

2 Paint the scrolls

Using a paint stirring stick, mix DecoArt Sandstones Golden Fleck with very small amounts of AquaColors Ochre Yellow, Earth Brown and Earth Green to create a yellow/green color. Use a large, round artist brush and a smooth fluid motion to paint the scrolls in a random fashion. The scrolls will dry darker than they appear when painting. Apply two layers. Let dry approximately four hours between the first and second layers and 24 hours before glazing.

Simply Scrolls

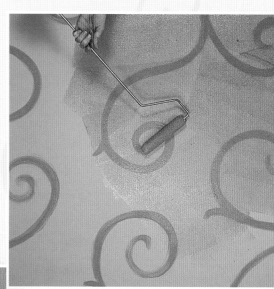
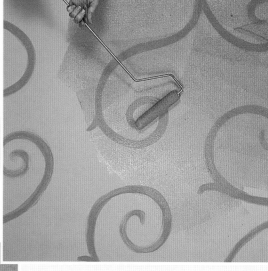

3 Apply glaze

Make a glaze by mixing one cup (23cl) of AquaCreme with three tablespoons (4cl) of each AquaColor. (The more AquaColor you add, the deeper your glaze color will be.) Follow the instructions for glazing a sealed surface on page 11. You will need to scrub the glaze into the scrolls in a curcular motion with your chip brush.

4 Soften the glaze

Take a dry terry cloth towel and rub in a circular motion to soften the color.

Embossing stencils is an elegant way to add interest to any room. The technique is easy and, what a relief, you don't have to draw or create your own design. Don't worry if the stencil area you create isn't exactly the same every time. In fact, it is the imperfections that add interest and create a distressed look. The results can be breathtaking.

royal relief

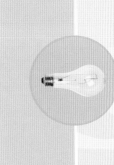

Supplies

- Paint roller and pan
- Pencil
- Level
- 3M Safe-Release tape
- Royal Design stencil #812 Toulouse
- Rapid-Bond Lite 90 Setting Type Joint Compound powder
- Drill and mixing attachment
- Buckets or other containers
- 2 Japan scrapers
- AquaGlaze
- 3-inch (76mm) chip brushes
- Terry cloth towels
- Porter Paint #6838-2 Antique Cream (satin)
- Porter Paint #6761-2 Post Oak (satin)

6838-2

#6761-2*

* Color shown as glaze/paint mix.

tip

When creating a wall finish with a raised surface, choose a stencil with only one overlay. It is difficult to add additional stenciling over the raised area just created.

1 Basecoat

Basecoat the walls with Antique Cream satin paint. Let dry 24 hours.

2 Prepare to stencil

Mark off the guides on the stencil, using a pencil and a level all the way around the room.

3 Stencil

Tape your stencil to the wall with Safe-Release tape. Using a small Japan scraper, trowel the drywall mud/Antique Cream paint mix (see page 10) onto the stencil to about ⅛-inch (3mm) thickness. Pull the stencil off carefully, pulling from the top of the stencil in a downward direction. Because your recently stenciled area is wet, skip over the next registration mark to the third registration mark to stencil again. Stencil around the room in this way. Let dry overnight before glazing.

Royal Relief

tip

When troweling drywall mud/paint mix through the stencil, don't press hard. Pretend that you are frosting a delicate cake.

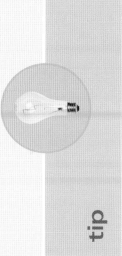

4 Apply paint/glaze mix

Mix three parts AquaGlaze with one part Post Oak paint. Take your chip brush and scrub the paint onto the stenciled wall area in a circular motion to get in all the nooks and grooves.

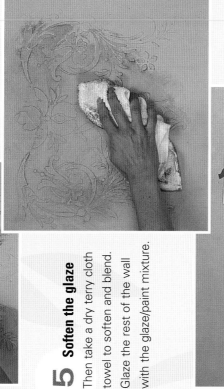

5 Soften the glaze

Then take a dry terry cloth towel to soften and blend. Glaze the rest of the wall with the glaze/paint mixture.

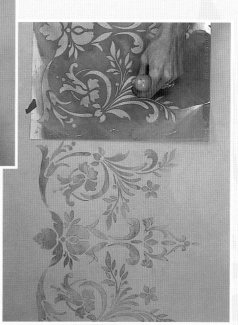

6 Darken the stenciled area

When the wall is dry, lay the stencil back over the raised stenciled area. Use a quick, circular motion with a stencil brush and the Post Oak (or an alternate color) glaze/paint mix to darken the stenciled area.

royal jewels

When I was working in India designing beaded gowns, I was taken with all the buildings decorated with inlaid designs, especially the Taj Mahal. They were amazingly beautiful, but it took hundreds of years to create these patterns.

This technique gives the look of inlaid jewels, but in a LOT less time!

Supplies

- Paint roller and pan
- Royal Design Studios stencil #812 Toulouse
- Pencil
- Level
- 3M Safe-Release tape
- Rapid-Bond Lite 90 Setting Type Joint Compound powder
- 2 Japan scrapers
- AquaGlaze
- 3-inch (76mm) chip brushes
- Terry cloth towels
- Assorted flat-back gems and jewels
- Porter Paint #6838-2 Antique Cream (satin)
- Porter Paint #6761-2 Post Oak (satin)

#6838-2

#6761-2*

* Color shown as glaze/paint mix.

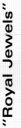

"Royal Jewels"

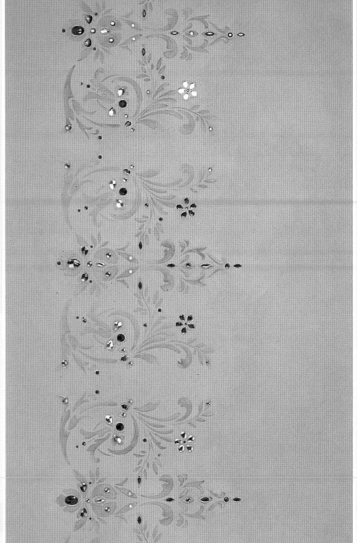

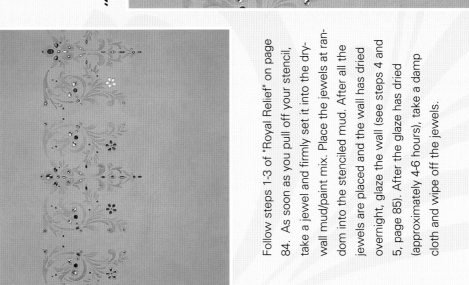

Follow steps 1-3 of "Royal Relief" on page 84. As soon as you pull off your stencil, take a jewel and firmly set it into the dry-wall mud/paint mix. Place the jewels at random into the stenciled mud. After all the jewels are placed and the wall has dried overnight, glaze the wall (see steps 4 and 5, page 85). After the glaze has dried (approximately 4-6 hours), take a damp cloth and wipe off the jewels.

sparkle & shine

To the artist's soul, there's nothing as beautiful, fluid and charming as something that is handpainted. Handpainting is faster for me than stenciling or using tape to create shapes. I use my tools as my guides—when I use a 1-inch (25mm) brush, then my stripes will be 1-inch wide. I use the curves and indentations of the molding to start and stop color. Use the same principle for adding trims and other embellishments.

Make your decorating projects as fun and easy as possible!

Home of Mark, Susan & Delaney Zink

Supplies

- Paint roller and pan
- Acrylic craft paint (white, yellow, peach, medium purple, green)
- Blender/extender
- Rags
- Level
- Pencil
- Ruler
- Flat artists brushes of various sizes, including 1-inch (25mm)
- Embellishments (beaded trim, flat-back roses, crystals)
- YES! paste
- Porter Paint #6542-1
- Pale Lavender (satin)

#6542-1

1 Basecoat

Basecoat your wall with Pale Lavender. Let dry 24 hours.

2 Paint stripes on molding

Load white and purple craft paint, with a bit of extender added, onto the brush. Using the width of the brush as a guide, handpaint stripes onto the molding. Have a damp rag handy to clean up any mistakes quickly. Don't aim for perfection! Use the same brush with the Pale Lavender wall paint and paint a hint of color in between the stripes you just painted, so the white stripes are not stark-looking.

3 Paint the lower molding

Paint across the lower portion of the molding with green and white craft paint and extender. Use a brush that matches the size of the section of the molding you're painting.

5 Paint swags

Using a level and a pencil, place a small mark every 12 inches (31cm) below the molding. Go back to the midpoint of the 12-inch (31cm) space, measure down 4 inches (10cm) from the bottom of the molding and make a small mark. Load the 1-inch (25mm) brush with Pale Lavender wall paint and purple and white craft paint. Paint free-form swags across each 12-inch (31cm) space, making the lowest point of the swag at the 4-inch (10cm) mark. Use fluid movements and add extender if necessary. Paint the swags around the room,

4 Paint checks

Next, dip into yellow craft paint, add a bit of extender, and paint small checks on the lowest part of the molding. When the yellow paint runs out, dip into the pink craft paint (don't forget to add some extender) and fill in the white spaces with the pink. Continue this all around the room.

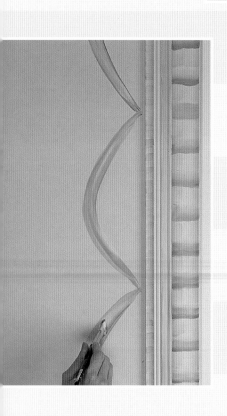

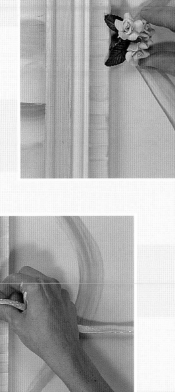

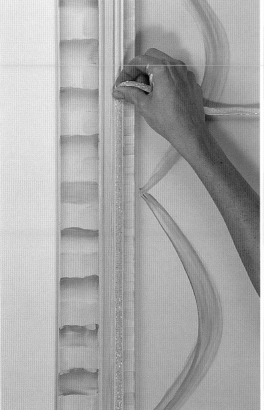

6 Add embellishments

Add embellishments of beaded trim, flat-back crystals and roses wherever you desire with YES! paste.

Sparkle & Shine

south of the border

This next border project proves that you are not limited to sparkles and roses. Embellishment knows no gender, age or design style. This technique uses colors and designs that are darker and a bit more masculine. Embellishment is added with dark, frosted marbles and silvery upholstery tacks. This border treatment is perfect for a home office or den, a tailored master bedroom or a bath.

Supplies

- Paint roller and pan
- 2-inch (51mm) 3M Safe-Release tape
- Level
- Pencil
- 2-inch (51mm) chip brushes
- Flat artists brushes of various sizies
- Rags
- Pewter iridescent squeeze paint
- Copper iridescent squeeze paint
- Upholstery tacks (silver)
- Red & frosted navy blue flat-back marbles
- YES! paste
- Porter Paint #7121-3 Hatteras Gray (satin)
- Porter Paint #6424-2 Cup Blue (satin)
- Porter Paint #7045-1 Pine Mist (satin)
- Porter Paint #6617-4 Dusty Grape (satin)
- Porter Paint #6522-5 Rich Navy (satin)
- Porter Paint #6102-3 Chutney (satin)
- Porter Paint #6927-2 Wood Laurel (satin)

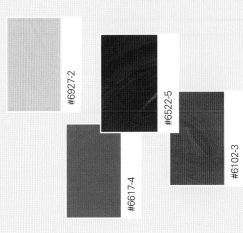

#6927-2

#6522-5

#6617-4

#6102-3

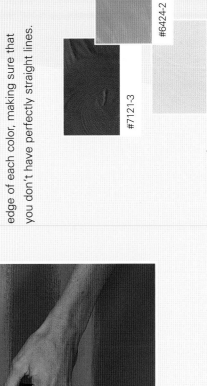

#7121-3

#6424-2

#7045-1

1 Basecoat

Basecoat the wall with Hatteras Gray. Let dry 24 hours.

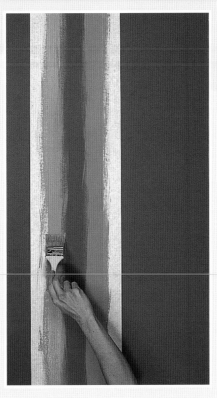

2 Tape off the border & start painting

Level and tape off the border area on the wall with 2-inch (51mm) 3M Safe-Release tape. Using the 2-inch (51mm) chip brush and Cup Blue, lightly paint a stripe the width of the brush along the bottom tape line. Use the same brush and Pine Mist (mixed occasionally into the Cup Blue paint) to lightly paint a line against the top tape line. Paint all around the room. Remove the tape.

3 Expand the border

Using the same brush and colors, paint along the top edge and the bottom edge of each color, making sure that you don't have perfectly straight lines.

4 Add more color

Using Dusty Grape, lightly paint next to the Cup Blue line of paint. Occasionally check for straightness with a level. Using an artist brush and Rich Navy, paint a stripe the same width as the brush below the Pine Mist stripe.

5 Add even more color

Using an artist brush and Chutney, paint a thin freehand line under the Cup Blue stripe.

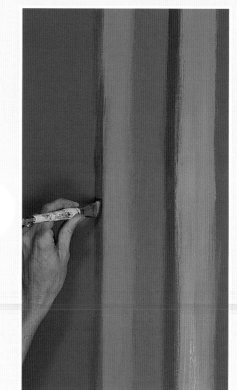

6 Paint dashes

Use a 1-inch (3mm) wide artist brush and Wood Laurel and paint dashes approximately 2 inches (5cm) long across the top.

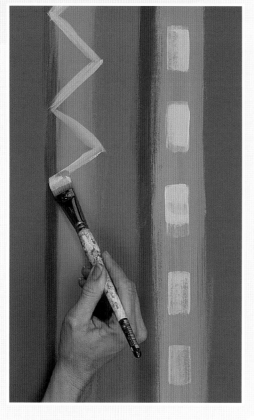

7 Paint zigzag lines

Using the same brush, dip into Pine Mist on one brush corner and Wood Laurel on the other brush corner. Paint a zigzag line starting at the very bottom of the border and going up into the Dusty Grape.

tip

If you hit a stud with the tack, just snip off the flat top of the tack with wire cutters and glue it on the wall with YES! paste.

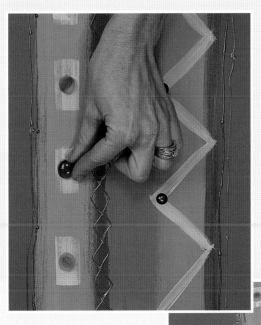

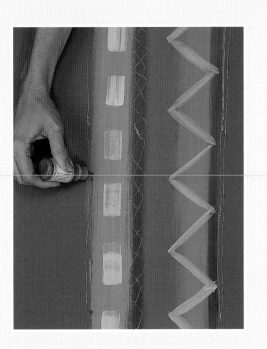

8 Apply embellishments

Drag a line of pewter squeeze paint along the very bottom of the border to outline. Then take the pewter squeeze paint and draw a zigzag design in the Rich Navy line. Use the copper squeeze paint to add additional accents. You don't have to follow these exact directions—be creative.

9 Apply tacks & marbles

When the paint is dry, take a level and a pencil and mark where you want to place the upholstery tacks. Place the tacks on the tip of the Pine Mist peaks. Then hammer them into the wall. Use YES! paste to attach the flat-back marbles into the Wood Laurel dashes on the wall.

South of the Border

shabby chic

I love pattern on pattern with more pattern! In this "Shabby Chic" project I used preprinted paper. But don't think that's the easy way out. It takes a lot of thought and creativity to combine colors, patterns and sizes to get just the right kind of "shabby" look. Lay out all your papers first and take a photo so that you have a guide.

Supplies

- Paint roller and pan
- Wallpaper sizing
- Assorted decorative papers (craft papers, scrapbook papers, wallpaper scraps, wrapping paper, photos)
- Scissors or paper cutter
- Clear wallpaper paste
- Rags and terry cloth towels
- Golden sparkle squeeze bottle paint
- Flat-back gems
- Porter Paint #6883-1 White Wheat (satin)

#6883-1

Shabby Chic

1 Size walls

Base the walls in White Wheat. Let dry. Make sure the walls are clean. Then size them with wallpaper size.

2 Cut decorative papers

Cut your decorative papers in different size squares and rectangles. Use a roller to apply clear wallpaper paste to the back of the papers and then randomly place them on the wall. Use a dry rag to smooth out any bubbles and a lightly damp terry cloth towel to wipe up excess paste. Immediately wipe off the moisture with a dry towel.

3 Embellish

Outline all the paper edges with golden sparkle paint. Place iridescent gems randomly on corners, etc.

checkmate

If you're a fan of torn paper, you'll love this project—the organic nature of the craft paper adds to the finish. And you can tear and cut the paper into any shape you desire to suit your room.

tip

To figure out how much paper you'll need for a room, measure the square footage and add 25 percent more. Example: 100 square feet (9sqm) of wall requires 125 square feet (12sqm) of paper.

The Montgomery Inn, Montgomery, Ohio

Supplies

- Paint roller and pan
- Terry cloth towels
- 3-inch (76mm) chip brushes
- Medium weight craft paper
- Spray bottle with water
- Medium weight craft paper
- Straight edge
- Pencil
- Clear wallpaper paste
- Porter Paint #6886-2
  Bassett Hall Gold (satin)
- Porter Paint #6065-6
  Garnet (satin)
- Porter Paint #6108-3
  Cinnamon Stick (satin)
- Porter Paint #6072-7
  Fire Engine Red (satin)
- Porter Paint #6096
  Accent Orange (satin)
- Modern Masters Metallic
  ME 200 Pale Gold
- Modern Masters Metallic
  ME 196 Pearl White
- Modern Masters Metallic
  ME 660 Pharoah's Gold

*Color shown as glaze/paint mix.

#6886-2

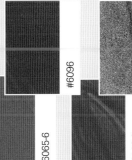

#6096

#6065-6

ME 200*

ME 196*

ME 660*

#6108-3

#6072-7

1 Basecoat

Basecoat the walls with Bassett Hall Gold. Let dry 24 hours.

2 Apply glaze mix

Make a glaze/paint mix with Modern Masters Pale Gold (see page 11). Roll the glaze/paint mix onto the wall. Then take a terry cloth towel to blend and soften the glaze. Work in sections and make sure to feather out and feather in. Let dry.

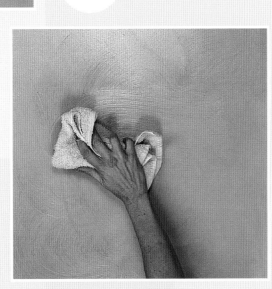

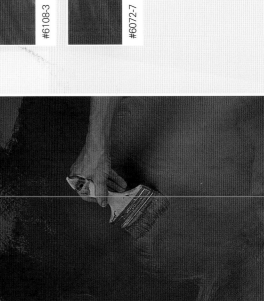

3 Apply colors on paper

Dip the 3-inch (8cm) chip brush into Fire Engine Red and just randomly brush it all over the craft paper. Do the same thing with Garnet, Cinnamon Stick and Accent Orange. Let a bit of the craft paper show through.

4 Create spatters

Spray the craft paper with water to help smear the paint and to create puddles, drips and smears. Splatter colors onto the paper with your chip brush, and then spritz with water to soften the splatters. Let dry completely.

5 Apply glazes

Make a mix of Modern Masters Pearl White and AquaGlaze (equal parts of each) and a mix of Modern Masters Pharoah's Gold and AquaGlaze (equal parts of each). Randomly spread both mixes over the paper.

6 Blend & soften the glazes

Take a terry cloth towel and blend and soften the glazes into the paper. Use a spray bottle with water and spritz the paper occasionally to make the glaze mixes easier to move around.

7 Create texture on paper

While the pearlescent glazes are wet, spray the water onto the paper and let it sit for a few minutes. Then pounce with a terry cloth towel that has been folded into a flat square. This creates pits and water marks.

8 Mist the paper

Before the paper is dry, mist with Krylon Metallic Enamel Gold. Adjust the pressure of the nozzle with your finger so that large drops spatter onto the paper. Hold the spray can about two feet (61cm) from the paper surface. Let dry.

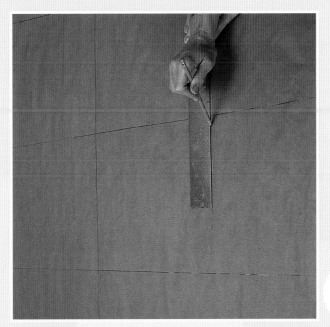

9 Mark square sizes

Turn the paper over and mark squares of the size you desire with a straight edge and pencil.

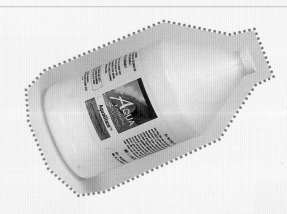

11 Apply the paper to the wall

Roll or brush clear wallpaper paste onto the back of the torn paper. Measure the wall and mark with a pencil where the torn paper should be placed. Place the pasted torn paper onto the wall.

10 Tear the paper

Follow the lines you've marked and start tearing the paper, holding the straight edge along the tear line. Don't try to achieve perfection; the paper should have a definite hand-torn look.

it's wall about fun

This is an original and interesting way to create a stone wall. You will find that it's a blast to paint the paper. And there is no measuring and taping off the wall! You've got to love those shortcuts!

You can find craft paper at your local craft store, paper supply company or a store that sells shipping supplies.

Supplies

- Paint roller and pan
- Medium weight craft paper
- 3-inch (76mm) chip brushes
- Spray bottle with water
- Terry cloth towels
- AquaGlaze
- Straight edge
- Pencil
- Scissors or craft knife
- Clear wallpaper paste
- Level
- ¼-inch (6mm) masking tape
- Porter Paint #6886-2
  Bassett Hall Gold (satin)
- Porter Paint #6900-3
  Autumn Bronze (satin)
- Porter Paint #6927-2
  Wood Laurel (satin)
- Porter Paint #6912-2
  Bur Oak (satin)
- Modern Masters Metallic
  ME 196 Pearl White
- Modern Masters Metallic
  ME 660 Pharoah's Gold

#6886-2

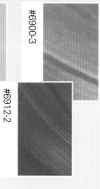

#6900-3

#6927-2

#6912-2

ME 196*

ME 660*

*Color shown as glaze/paint mix.

1 Basecoat

Basecoat the walls with Bassett Hall Gold. Let dry 24 hours.

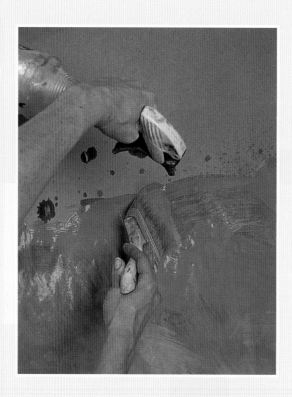

2 Create color & texture on paper

Take a 3-inch (76mm) chip brush with Autumn Bronze and spread it randomly all over the craft paper. Do the same thing with Wood Laurel and Bur Oak. Let some of the craft paper show through in spots. Take a water bottle and spritz the painted paper, allowing the colors to run and drip. Blend the colors with a brush and terry cloth towel. Finally, take the chip brush and spray drops of color all over. Soften these drops of color with a spritz of water, if needed. Let dry completely.

4 Create more texture

While the pearlescent glaze is still wet, take a spray bottle with water and spritz the surface of the paper. Let it sit for a few minutes. Then take a terry cloth towel, fold it into a flat square and pounce the surface of the paper. You will be able to see the imprints of the water drops. Let the paper dry completely.

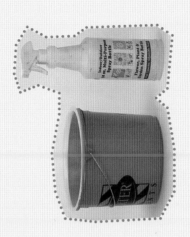

5 Measure & mark rectangle shapes

Turn the paper over and mark the rectangles, using a straight edge and pencil. The approximate size of the rectangles is 12" x 8" (30cm x 20cm).

3 Apply glaze

Mix Modern Masters Pearl White and AquaGlaze (equal parts of each) and mix Modern Masters Pharoah's Gold and AquaGlaze (equal parts of each). Use your chip brush and spread both mixes randomly over the dried craft paper. Then soften and blend with a terry cloth towel.

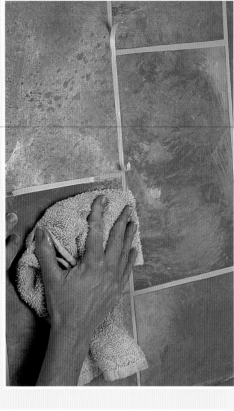

7 Apply the paper to the wall

Use a roller or brush to apply wallpaper paste to the back of the paper. Apply the paper to the wall, always checking with your level to make sure it is even. Starting at the center of the paper, smooth it out using a terry cloth towel to eliminate any air bubbles that may appear. Start at the ceiling, working from the middle of the wall toward the side walls. Once you have your first row, you can alternate your stone blocks accordingly. Use small strips of ¼-inch (6mm) masking tape as a guide for the width of your "grout" lines by placing them on the side of each block. Line up your next block to the outside edge of the tape. Remove the tape and move to the next section.

6 Cut out the rectangles

Use scissors or a craft knife and a straight edge to cut out the rectangles along the marked lines. After you get the hang of it, you can cut a few layers at once.

It's Wall About Fun

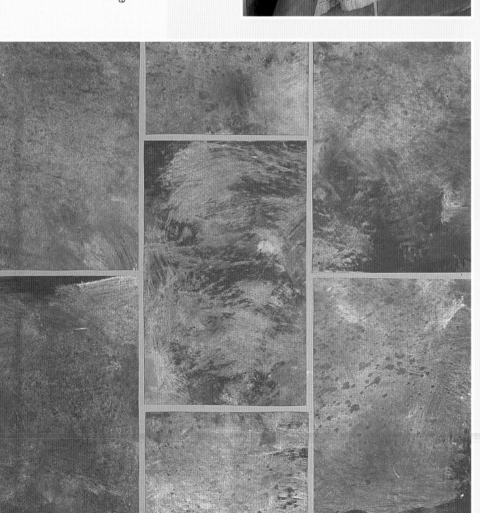

it's a delicate tissue

This technique seems so simple—and it is. But you need careful planning and patience, because tissue paper is delicate.

Use same-color tissue paper for a tone-on-tone look or create a rainbow room using several different colors. This treatment not only adds color, but also slight texture to your walls.

Supplies

- Paint roller and pan
- Wallpaper sizing
- Craft glue
- Water
- Purple tissue paper sheets
- 6-inch (15cm) foam roller and tray
- AquaSeal, or any other water-based clear sealer
- AquaGlaze
- Terry cloth towels
- Porter Paint 6542-1 Pale Lavender (satin)
- Modern Masters Metallic Pearl White ME196

6542-1

ME196*

*Color shown as glaze/paint mix.

1 Basecoat & size walls

Basecoat walls with Pale Lavender. Size the walls with wallpaper sizing. Let dry 24 hours.

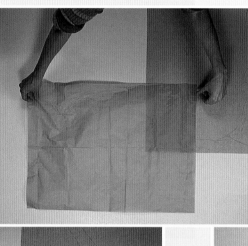

2 Apply tissue paper to the wall

Mix craft glue with water (60 percent glue to 40 percent water). Roll this mixture on the wall in a section that is larger than the paper you'll be placing on the wall. Place paper on the wall (starting at the ceiling-level corner). Then roll back over it with your wet roller. Place your next pieces overlapping the other pieces.

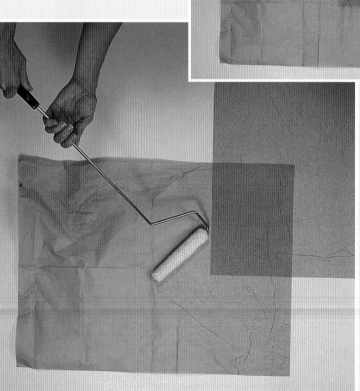

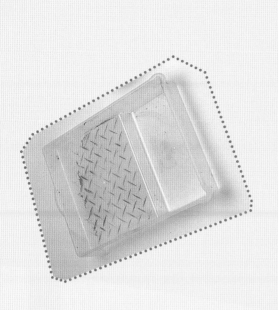

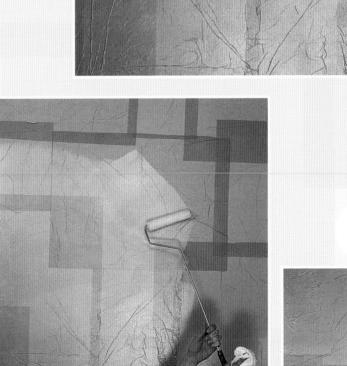

It's a Delicate Tissue

3 Apply more tissue paper

Just keep applying paper, overlapping and covering the entire wall. Cut your tissue paper in smaller squares or rectangles to fit into corners, etc. To avoid tearing the paper, roll off excess glue/water mixture in the paint roller pan before rolling over tissue paper on the wall

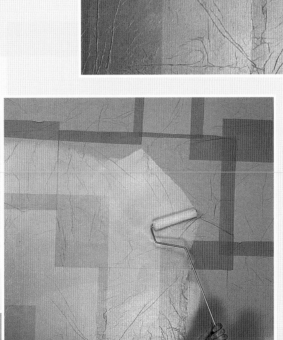

4 Apply clear sealer & glaze

After all the paper is applied, let dry for 24 hours. Then roll a clear sealer over the surface. When dry, mix three parts AquaGlaze with one part Modern Masters Pearl White paint. Roll the glaze/paint mixture over the tissue paper wall.

5 Soften the glaze

Lightly rub the glaze with a terry cloth towel to soften.

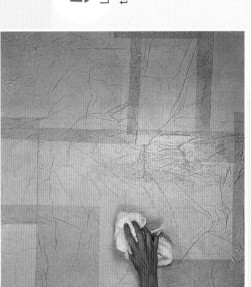

oyster bay

Every time I see an oyster, I marvel at the thought of a beautiful pearl being made inside its rugged shell. I always secretly wish to find a pearl inside, resting in its pure, natural state. But since that never happens, I guess faux pearls are really for me!

"Oyster Bay" walls give you that beautiful, luxuriant luminescence of a pearl. But beware. This wall treatment must be used where little hands won't be tempted to pluck the pearl from its shell!

Oyster Bay

Off White

Pearl

Supplies

- Paint roller and pan
- Venetian trowel
- Metal or plastic trowel
- Faux pearls, any size
- AquaBond Off White
- Aqua Palette Art Pearl

1 Basecoat

Basecoat the walls with two coats of Neutral White AquaBond. Let dry 24 hours.

2 Apply Palette Art Pearl

Trowel on a thick layer of Palette Art Pearl. Make sure to apply the Palette Art as thickly as you would frosting on a cake.

3 Apply pearls

While the walls are still wet, place your pearls onto the wall at random. If you're using beading pearls, make sure the holes are on the sides as you place the pearls onto the Palette Art wall.

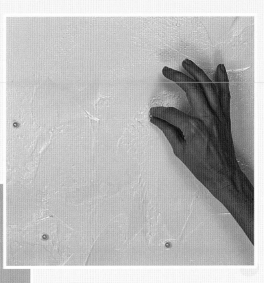

mermaid stripes

You can never go wrong with stripes, especially when this classic design has a creative and surprising twist. With beautiful soft colors, fluid scrolls and floating jewels, your room will be as pretty as a mermaid. Because of the large number of patterns and embellishments you'll be placing on your wall, this treatment is perfect for small spaces.

Supplies

- Paint roller and pan
- Level
- 2-inch (51mm) 3M Safe-Release tape
- AquaGlaze
- 3-inch (76mm) chip brushes
- Terry cloth towels
- Duncan Scribbles 3-D craft paint, SC201 White Mist
- Credit card or other hard plastic edge
- Assorted flat-back gems and jewels
- Porter Paint #6493-1 Pale Frost (satin)
- Porter Paint #6556-2 Grape Tint (satin)
- Porter Paint #6609-2 Stratus Gray (satin)

#6493-1

#6556-2*

#6609-2*

*Color shown as glaze/paint mix.

1 Basecoat

Basecoat the walls with Pale Frost. Let dry 24 hours.

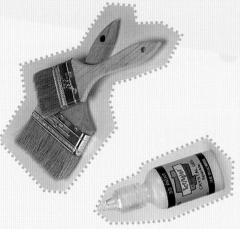

2 Tape off the stripes

Measure and tape off 6-inch (15cm) wide stripes. Burnish the edges of the tape with a credit card or hard-edge piece of plastic so the glazes will not seep underneath.

3 Paint the stripes

mixes of two parts AquaGlaze to one part of each paint color (Grape Tint and Stratus Gray). Use a 3-inch (76mm) chip brush and paint random strokes of Grape Tint glaze and Stratus Gray glaze on the stripes you have taped off.

4 Blend & soften colors

Use a dry terry cloth towel to blend and soften the colors. Continue painting and blending all around the room. Let dry thoroughly. Pull off the tape.

tip

Use the width of your tape as a measuring tool. When making 6-inch (15cm) stripes, always use 2-inch (51mm) tape, tearing three strips that are placed next to each other.

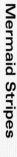

5 Embellish the stripes

Use the squeezable Scribbles craft paint and make fluid scrolls along the painted stripes. While the scrolls are wet, apply the jewels and gems at random into the Scribbles paint on the wall.

Mermaid Stripes

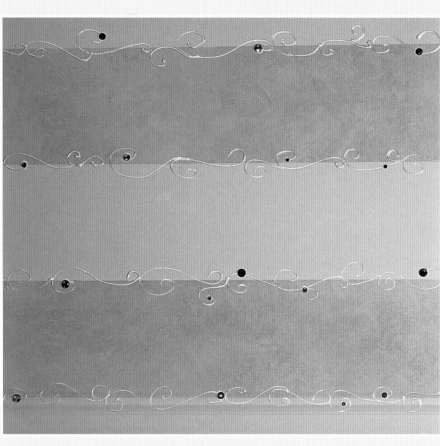

relish & embellish

Do you have an ugly support column in your basement? Use all your leftover baubles and trinkets to create a mosaic masterpiece. You'll be amazed at how wonderfully this turns out, especially if you use found objects that have meaning to you and your family. Embellish with mementos you have collected on vacations and trips. Use old silver spoons, coins, broken china pieces or broken pieces of costume jewelry. Set a theme and go with it!

The Dostal Home

Supplies

- Marble gems
- Decorative ceramic tiles
- Seashells
- Marbles
- Beads and pearls
- Old silverware
- Old jewelry
- Tile mortar
- Grout (any color)
- Plastic gloves
- Water
- Sponges

Dip your embellishment items (beads, tiles, etc.) into a generous amount of tile mortar and then apply to the column. Start at the top of the column and work your way down. When the column is completely embellished, let dry overnight. Mix the grout (color of your choice). Using plastic gloves, pick up small golf-ball size handfuls of grout and squeeze it in between your embellished items on the column. Do this until you've grouted the entire column. Wipe off the excess grout with a damp sponge.

tree of life

Some beautiful motifs and ornamental designs date back thousands of years. I look for books and artwork that feature classic designs and study them for ideas and inspiration. A designer I work with introduced me to this particular ancient Etruscan motif found on vases in the Louvre. I used the basic design but added the marble gems for an extra twist. You can do the same thing. Make something old new again!

Supplies

- Paint roller and pan
- AquaGlaze
- 3-inch (76mm) chip brushes
- Terry cloth towels
- Chalk
- Terry cloth towels
- Artist brush
- Flat-back marble accents (or any flat-back gems) in assorted colors
- YES! paste
- Porter Paint #7045-1 Pine Mist (satin)
- Modern Masters Metallic ME 249 Teal
- Modern Masters Metallic ME 247 Sage
- Modern Masters Metallic ME 661 Tequila Gold

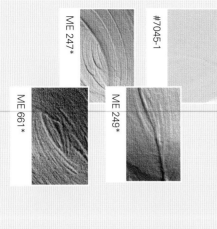

#7045-1

ME 247*

ME 249*

ME 661*

*Color shown as glaze/paint mix.

1 Basecoat

Basecoat walls with two coats of Pine Mist. Let dry for 24 hours.

2 Apply glaze

Mix three parts AquaGlaze with one part of each Modern Masters color. Use the chip brush to apply colors to your wall in a random fashion.

3 Blend colors

Use a terry cloth towel to rub and blend the colors together. Let dry 24 hours before moving on to the next step.

5 Paint the tree shape

Mix together equal parts of Tequila Gold and AquaGlaze. Use an artist brush to paint over the chalk tree shape. The tree shape can be as sheer or opaque as you like; you control that with the layers of paint applied.

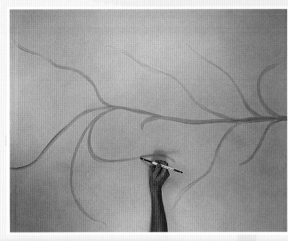

4 Draw the tree shape

Using light pressure, draw the tree shape on the wall with chalk. If you're not happy with what you've drawn, wipe it off with a rag.

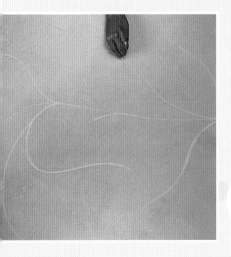

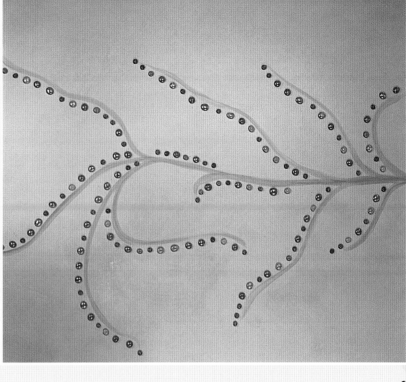

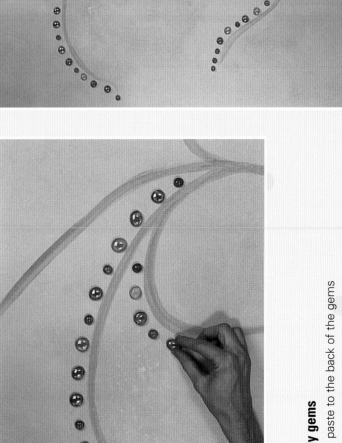

6 Apply gems

Apply YES! paste to the back of the gems and place them along the tree branches. Vary the colors as you paste them on.

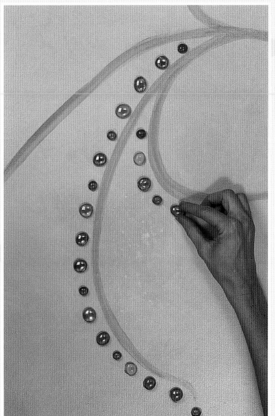

Tree of Life

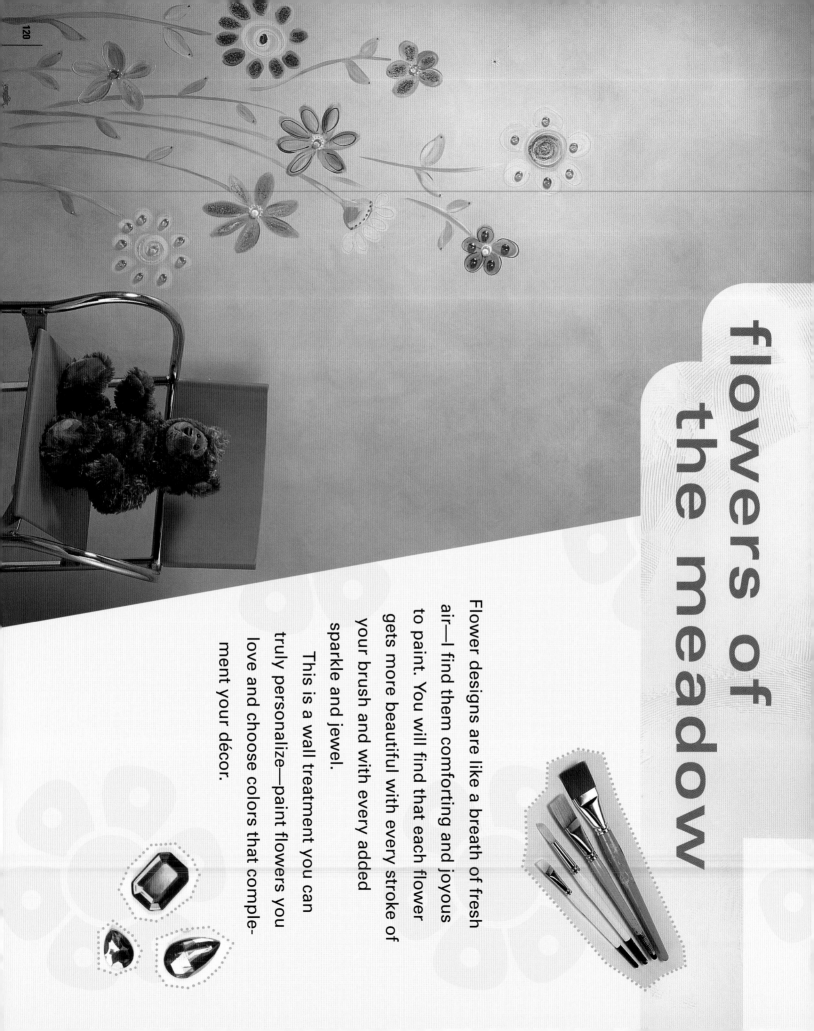

flowers of the meadow

Flower designs are like a breath of fresh air—I find them comforting and joyous to paint. You will find that each flower gets more beautiful with every stroke of your brush and with every added sparkle and jewel.

This is a wall treatment you can truly personalize—paint flowers you love and choose colors that complement your décor.

Supplies

- Paint roller and pan
- AquaGlaze
- 3-inch (76mm) chip brushes
- Terry cloth towels
- Acrylic craft paints
  in a variety of colors
- Various artist brushes
- YES! paste
- Gems
- Glitter glue
- 3-D paint
- Porter Paint #6493-1
  Pale Frost (satin)
- Porter Paint #6556-2
  Grape Tint (satin)
- Porter Paint #6609-2
  Stratus Gray (satin)
- Porter Paint #7195-1
  White Umber (satin)

#6493-1

#6556-2*

#6609-2*

#7195-1*

*Color shown as glaze/paint mix.

tip

Practice painting your flowers on poster board before painting them on the wall.

1 Basecoat

Basecoat your walls with Pale Frost. Let dry for 24 hours.

2 Apply glaze

Mix three parts AquaGlaze to one part paint (Grape Tint, Stratus Gray and White Umber) to create your glaze colors. Use a 3-inch (76mm) chip brush to apply colors randomly on the wall.

122

3 Blend colors

Use a terry cloth towel to blend paint colors and create a soft background.

tip

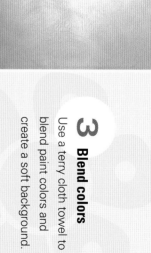

Double load your brush by loading the first paint color on one side of the brush and a second color on the other side. Here you see a double load of two shades of pink acrylic craft paint. All your flower colors should be double-loaded.

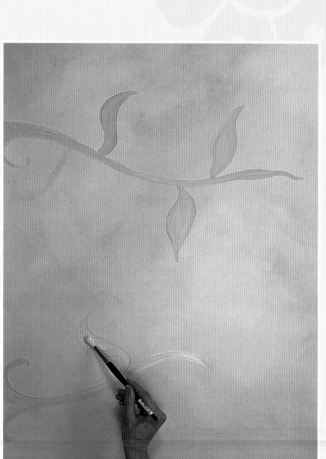

4 Paint stems & leaves

Double load (see tip on this page) your paint brush with two shades of green acrylic craft paint. Paint all the stems and leaves. Keep your movements fluid and paint with a whimsical touch.

5 Paint flowers

Use fluid movements to paint flowers and petals. Keep the design simple. Let paint dry before moving on to the next step.

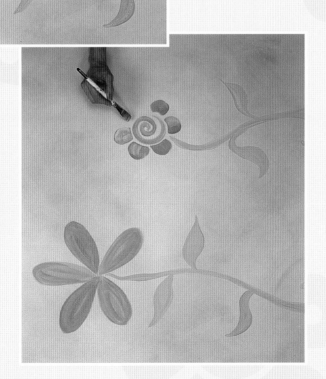

6 Embellish the flowers

Use YES! paste, gems, glitter glue, 3-D paint and your creativity to embellish the painted flowers. Apply the sparkles first, as directed in "It's All Aglitter," steps 4 and 5, on page 49.

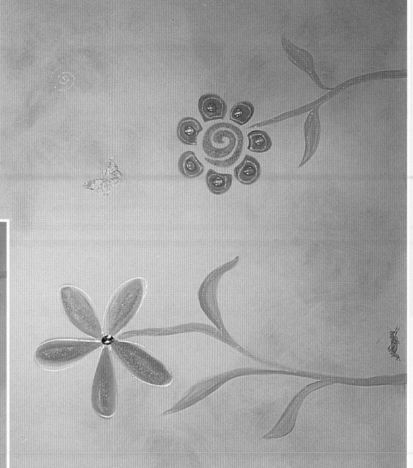

tip

If you're not happy with your painted flowers, remember they'll look great after they've been jeweled and sparkled.

Flowers of the Meadow

"extreme makeover" cutouts

If you haven't discovered wallpaper cutouts yet, here is your introduction. I've used them for several years and I love them. They're designed by artists, then printed on special paper and applied like wallpaper. As beautiful as they are on their own, once embellished, they really come to life. But don't limit them to walls—you can apply them to just about any surface. So, "make over" some wallpaper cutouts—I wish I could get an extreme makeover this easily!

Extreme MakeOver Wallpaper Cutouts

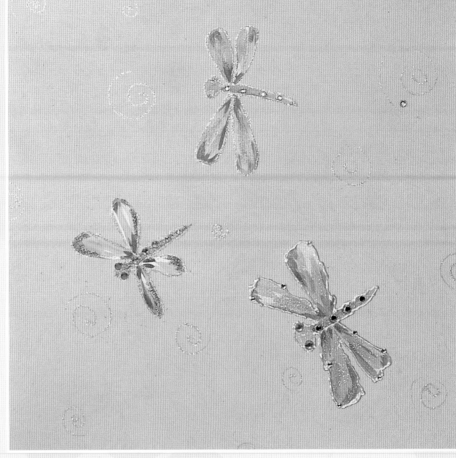

Supplies

- Wallpaper cutouts
- Any gems, sparkles and other embellishments
- 3-M Safe-Release tape (if necessary)
- YES! paste

1 Prep the wall

You can apply any type of finish to the wall surface before applying wallpaper cutouts. Make sure walls are dry and clean. Place your cutouts onto the wall according to the manufacturer's directions.

2 Embellish cutouts

Be creative when embellishing your cutouts. Make a trough (see page 49) to catch falling glitter and sparkles. Add jewels for eyes.

paint

DecoArt Sandstone
DecoArt, Inc.
P.O. Box 386
Stanford, KY 40484
www.decoart.com
800-367-3047

Aqua Products
Faux Effects International, Inc.
3535 Aviation Blvd.
Vero Beach, FL 32960
www.fauxfx.com
800-270-8871

OR

Prismatic Painting Studio
935 W. Galbraith Rd.
Cincinnati, OH 45231
www.prismaticpainting.com
513-931-5520

Modern Masters, Inc.
13201 Saticoy St.
Hollywood, CA 91605
www.modernmastersinc.com
800-942-3166

Porter Paint
400 South 13th St.
Louisville, KY 40201
www.porterpaints.com
866-823-2585

other materials

Cake decorating bags and tips
Wilton Industries
2240 W. 75th Street
Woodridge, IL 60517
www.wilton.com
800-794-5866

Copper leaf and metal leaf size
Houston Art
10770 Moss Ridge Road
Houston, TX 77043-1175
www.houstonart.com
800-272-3804

Gel medium
Golden Artist Colors, Inc.
188 Bell Rd.
New Berlin, NY 13411-9527
www.goldenpaints.com
800-959-6543

Butterfly stencil
Laser Excel
P.O. Box 279
N. 6323 Berlin Rd.
Green Lake, WI 54941
www.laserexcel.com
800-285-6544

Liquitex Modeling Paste
Liquitex
www.liquitex.com
888-422-7954

Available at most hardware stores or contact:

Rapid Bond Lite 90 Setting Type Joint Compound powder
Available at most hardware stores or contact:
Welco Mfg. Co.
P.O. Box 12568
North Kansas City, MO 64116
www.wel-cote.com
800-821-7352

Stencils
Royal Design Studio
2504 Transportation Ave., Suite H
National City, CA 91950
www.royaldesignstudio.com
800-747-9767

YES! Paste
Available at craft stores or through online craft and art sup-pliers

3M Safe-Release Painters' Masking Tape
Available at most hardware stores or contact:
3M
3M Center
St. Paul, MN 55144-1000
www.3m.com
888-364-3577

Wallpaper cutouts
Available at craft stores or through online craft and art sup-pliers

index

The best in home decorating instruction and inspiration is from North Light Books!

It's Faux Easy with Gary Lord

Let the master of faux finishing, Gary Lord, be your guide in creating fabulous faux finishes to accent your home's beauty. With Gary's easy-to-follow instructions, you'll learn how to create a variety of contemporary and traditional effects from dimensional plaster finishes with embossed or embedded stenciling to faux finishes with holographic or metallic flourishes. 30 unique finishes in all. It's easy with a master by your side!

ISBN 1-58180-554-3, paperback, 144 pages, #33010

Painting Borders for Your Home with Donna Dewberry

Donna shows you how to use her renowned one-stroke method to create colorful borders that give character and style to every room in your home. Coordinating borders accompany each project, so you can make perfect accessories. With photos showing the borders in actual homes, you'll find the inspiration you need to create master-pieces for walls and furniture through-out the house.

ISBN 1-58180-600-0, paperback, 128 pages, #33125

Painted Illusions: Create Stunning Trompe L'oeil Effects with Stencils

Add incredible beauty and elegance to your home with Painted Illusions. Even if you've never painted before, you can achieve professional-quality results with these simple stencil techniques and Melanie Royals' easy-to-follow direction. In 19 step-by-step projects, you'll learn to create beautiful wall finishes that mimic fabrics such as linen, silk and damask as well as trompe l'oeil effects such as leather, porcelain, oak paneling, granite, carved stone, and more.

ISBN 1-58180-548-9, paperback, 128 pages, #32899

Painting Murals Fast & Easy

Discover a quick and easy way to paint gorgeous wall murals. With just a common household sponge and acrylic paint, you can create landscapes, seascapes, still lifes and more. Find out how fun muraling can be! With hundreds of full-color step-by-step photos and clear instruction, you'll learn muralists Terrence and Theodore Tse's innovative techniques in no time. No expensive equipment or painting experience required!

ISBN 1-58180-573-X, paperback, 128 pages, #33030